HIS POWER

*Whisperings
Of God
Through
An Ardent
Listener*

Miriam Grosjean

D1159499

Dedicated to "Mary's House," the new
Our Lady of the Holy Spirit Center in Norwood, Ohio
and to all the volunteers working so diligently
to restore the Old St. Mary's Seminary complex.

This book is published by Our Lady of Light Publications, a subsidiary of Our Lady of Light Foundation, a tax exempt association. Our Lady of Light Foundation is a religious public charitable Gospa ministry association organized to foster support for Our Lady of Light Ministries.

For additional copies, write to:
Our Lady of Light Publications
P.O. Box 17541
Fort Mitchell, KY 41017

First OLLP Printing: September 1993
    Second Printing: January 1994
        Third Printing: September 1994
    Fourth Printing: April 1997

About the cover photo:
The original print of this famous image first surfaced mysteriously in a group of photographs taken in 1982 by a Scranton, Pa. couple on a visit to the Holy Land. Called the "True Image of Jesus" by many, it presents a striking visage of Jesus, one that fits the gentle, loving authority which accompanies His Power. This image has been reproduced and distributed by the tens of thousands throughout the world. It appears here with the permission of the original "owners." At their request, their names have not been used.

"...and how very great is His power at work in us who believe. This power working in us is the same as the mighty strength which He used when He raised Christ from death and seated Him at His right side in the heavenly world."

—Ephesians 1: 19-20

Table of Contents

Gratitude

Thanks to the Holy Spirit for choosing me as one of His messengers to enlighten others concerning His power. I sincerely hope these words, considered in the light of love, will draw the reader to a higher level of holiness.

Appreciation

With joy, I extend my appreciation to my friends who encouraged me to keep on writing. Their enthusiasm to hear what the Holy Spirit was conveying to me was most gratifying. Due to their urgings, I dared not fail them or other of God's people who are so open to the truly spiritual aspects of their faith.

Front of the old Mt. St. Mary Seminary, "Mary's House," newly reconsecrated as Our Lady of the Holy Spirit Center.

Charismatic healing service at "Mary's House," Our Lady of the Holy Spirit Center, Norwood, Ohio. Sponsored by the Gospa Group of Our Lady of Light Ministries.

Author's Forward

Just as everything in the universe is diversified, so too is the Lord's power. It is awesome and wonderful to behold. The following pages explore that wonder, if only in the way it affects us and people like us. The infinity of His whole and pervasive power is for the ages to discern and for Him to define in His own measure of time.

Publisher's Preface

The author of this book might be called a receiver since she does 'hear' the messages you are about to read. She hears them in sentence form, then transcribes them, sentence by sentence, to the best of her ability. Some might call her a locutionist. She states, firmly but graciously, however, that she is not the author. God is.

Whether or not you believe Miriam Grosjean is a 'receiver' or 'locutionist' or 'listener' is not important. Read the messages for their own merit. Then consider whether the source is human or divine. The importance is, after all, in the message itself and in its impact on the reader. If the impact is positive, and to most readers so far it has been, then in one way or another the words have been God-sent and we as readers should be grateful that God has given us these suggestions for our own spiritual development. If these be nearly literal directions from God, we should ponder His intent in voicing them, treasure them in our minds and hearts, then act on them.

If these messages uplift the spirit, and the publisher is convinced that they do, then the process of absorbing these spiritual hints involves the working of the Holy Spirit. The publisher asks the reader to pray to the Holy Spirit for the fulfillment of His Will in this regard.

Only God knows His intentions for the creatures He has fashioned. Throughout the history of the Church, from the apostles' time to the present, there have been reports of private revelations. Some of these reports concern visits from His Blessed Mother, some from angels and saints, and some even from God Himself. Receptors of such revelations have been people from a whole gamut of backgrounds, from high and low stations in life. What they have seen and heard has varied as widely as the persons and the times but one common thread through them all seems to be that the message, not the messenger, is what counts.

Today a crescendo of voices from 'messengers of God' seems to be coming from all parts of our world. From Venezuela, from Yugoslavia, from Russia—maybe even from Dayton, Ohio, U.S.A.—it's almost as if Someone is earnestly after our attention. Almighty God and His mother seem to be touching us more often and more intensely than ever before, offering help. Their messages are clear and consistent. They ask us to focus on prayer and penance, to work on growth in His Spirit. They've done that in other times, but in our time there seems to be a difference. This time there seems to be a special urgency, as if something might be up.

This book, addressing as it does such matters as angels, devils, visionary and healing power, is not for faith minimalists. It is for those who believe God's promise of giving us strength in proportion to need. Perhaps the contents of this book will remind them of the arsenal at their disposal for dealing with life's problems and with the difficult job of growing in Him amidst the growing distractions of a world askew.

This book is not structured in an essay pattern, one sentence locked to and anteceding another. Rather, this is a compendium of Godly thoughts, directed at common sense holiness, with related "power" concepts grouped under appropriate chapter themes. Each message is like a small burst of Spirit to the reader. They bring Him alive — brightly, uniquely in each man's eye. They offer a reflection of the power of God in mankind in a way not easy to compare with any other source. The messages don't just inform the soul. Rather, they elevate the spirit, the heart, and that's important to man so starved today in search of the Spirit of God. They give warm counsel about handling the everyday. As hints for living these gifts of insight are as soothing to the spirit as they are practical to the intellect. The quiet voices of the Three seem to be pulling the reader gently toward holiness, toward oneness with the One.

The Publisher

About The Author

Miriam Grosjean is the mother of four grown sons. A daily Communicant for most of her life, she worked as a secretary in Dayton, Ohio until her retirement in 1982.

About fifteen years ago Miriam was awakened at night to the sound of a single sentence of scripture being repeated over and over. Finally, she decided to write it down. Other sentences followed. The next morning she began to wonder if the whole episode had all been a dream but soon found the paper on which she had written her notes. Sandwiched between the scriptural passages, in her own handwriting, were the words, "You are my jewel." She could not remember writing that so she prayed for discernment. The messages continued.

After many messages, most of them received as she lay in bed at night, Miriam promised to publish them if Our Lord would give them to her daily. Printed here are messages received concerning the various aspects of God's Power. These elegantly simple messages speak to our inner selves in our intuitive, almost driven search for the glorious source of all power...God Himself.

Prayer to the Holy Spirit*

Come, Holy Spirit, fill the hearts of Your faithful and enkindle in them the fire of Your love.

V. Send forth Your Spirit and they shall be created,

R. And You shall renew the face of the earth.

Let us pray:
O, God, who by the light of the Holy Spirit, did instruct the hearts of Your faithful, grant that by that same Holy Spirit we may be truly wise and ever rejoice in His consolation, through Christ our Lord. Amen.

*This prayer is presented in the fervent hope that the reader asks the Holy Spirit for the gift of true listening before each and every reading of this book's messages.

His Introduction

To be effective in any ministry, you need My power. This comes through the Holy Spirit. I send the Holy Spirit to dwell in My faithful ones—those who repent of their sins and ask forgiveness. This power can keep one sinless. Without this power one will inevitably fall. Those who have this power recognize it in others. They have been likened to true discernment.

Without power in preaching your words do little to change others. Without power in the healing ministry any method you use will not bring results. To try to evangelize without power is a useless task. To prophesy without power brings only words of little value and truth. It is the Holy Spirit power that brings success to any ministry. I urge My people to pray and seek this power. It should be your greatest want in your present life.

Those who have been given signs of a ministry must keep in preparation for greater days to come. The body must be in good health to withstand My power. The soul should be kept pure and undefiled. All worldly vices must vanish. The will to serve should total one hundred percent. Then patience to wait on Me is extremely necessary. Pray in the interim and My grace will sustain you. Live in a normal fashion and stay humble for this is well pleasing to Me. Be a continual light in the darkened world.

Each one's days are numbered so they should be lived to the fullest. Pleasing the flesh will keep one from growing spiritually. Migrate in the spirit and you will not fulfill the lust of the flesh. Tap into My power for safekeeping.

My ways are mysterious but elevating. Fear not the unknown. Relax completely in My care with a willingness to serve. Let Me raise you from your lowly state into My heights. Your transformation will ever keep you amazed. Your quality of living will display My high standards.

My people should be aware of My power available to them. They perish from lack of knowledge. If they would hunger and thirst for righteousness, they would increase their knowledge. They should pray for enlightenment and I will answer their prayer.

By living a life of holiness My power is given out in diversified ways. Those who are open to it will receive according to My goodness and mercy. Their lives will be forever blessed.

Chapter 1
Almighty Power

My almighty power created the world. I spoke and called into being things that were not. This is how creation started. Read the first book in the Bible proving My almighty power.

※

One has only to observe nature to realize that a supreme being is in control of the universe. Look around for yourself and name the great wonders. Take a flower and discover the perfect symmetry, color, and beauty — all made through the power of My word.

※

The human being is a perfect example of My creation. The anatomy, with all its intricate parts, works in perfect harmony — all of this created through My power. Notice every face has two eyes, a nose, and a mouth. Yet every face looks different. Only a supreme designer could create such variety.

※

Animals are another species upon which to ponder. A wide variety could be named by all. Some are tamed for pets for human pleasure. Birds give out sounds pleasing to the ears and add beauty and life to the surroundings.

※

Trees are beautiful and give out shade. Grass is pleasing to the eye. No one can deny that nature was made for people's enjoyment. The mountains and hills add variety, along with the seasons.

※

If My people would slow down, they could reason for themselves how all was brought forth with My almighty power. Woe to those who do not acknowledge My existence. My wrath will come upon them. I have given them numerous chances but they curse the ground that they walk upon. My same almighty power will send them to the pit of hell.

Those who fear Me shall live for they follow My commands and statutes. Blessed are those who seek out righteousness. I will help all those who call upon Me. My Son redeemed the world through His suffering and death. Repent and believe in Him and you shall be saved. The words must come out of *your* lips and from *your* heart.

My Son will have My almighty power to judge both the living and the dead on Judgment Day when He will descend again to earth. Those who have been living a holy life will have nothing to fear. They will obtain everlasting life with gifts poured upon them from My storehouse. They will be robed in white garments that will dazzle the eyes. The majesty and splendor is too glorious for the human mind to comprehend.

My almighty power controls all the elements of the world. Many have yet to be discovered. I will reveal secrets to those who know My voice and stay close to Me in thought and deed. They will become winners for all eternity.

No discovery just happens. I am the force behind it to make it happen. Some people take control of discoveries for evil purposes but woe to them on judgment day. Man must control the knowledge obtained and use it for the good of all humankind. Otherwise they will be doomed. People in charge have a moral obligation to Me.

The weather is controlled by My almighty power. Atmospheric conditions were put there by Me. Man can go so far with knowledge but unless I open up new avenues, he is left in limbo. Each person's relationship with Me will make a difference. If that person believes in My almighty power, I will unleash facts for greater truths.

My almighty power will ever be. It always was and always will be. My words are the energy that supplies the power. The light which radiates from My being is shown brightly throughout the heavens. No human eyes can look upon My countenance because they were not created to withstand such light. You cannot fathom all of My wonders. Now it is like looking through a dark glass but the time will come when all will be made known to those who believe and follow My statutes.

Content yourself with the spiritual facts which I reveal to you. You are rich in that your faith causes you to believe more than your counterparts. Praise and magnify Me and I will take you from glory to glory. Those who doubt lose out on the excitement of these latter days.

My wisdom is not being held back from you because you are open to My Spirit. When you willingly acknowledge Me before your fellow men, I will acknowledge you in My Kingdom, reserving a special place just for you. Your hope is the human power that keeps you going. Those with no hope are dead already. My life in you will keep you alive for your crossover into My Kingdom. Look forward to it with heartfelt animation.

My almighty power keeps your world going around and suspends it in space. The stars are all numbered and controlled. There is nothing in the galaxy that was not directed and created by Me. The forces from My power keep you steady and hold everything in place. Without this power there would be no earth or creation.

Those who seek My power in prayerful submission will be satisfied. I neglect not My faithful ones. I am omnipotent and all-present to everyone who chooses My presence. Those who pay no heed to My presence miss out on My blessings in their present life. Joy comes from the inward knowing of this presence. Hope is a constant source of gladness which your faith, being renewed day by day, has developed. Spiritual gifts continue to grow as you draw closer to Me. I aid you in unknown ways. Your trials are stepping stones to My Kingdom.

My grace strengthens you for each one of them. Praise and thank Me and My power will be given you for certain works to glorify Me.

It is a pleasure to use My power for the good of My people. Those who understand My workings never cease thanking Me. The ungrateful receive little recompense from Me. I know every thought taking place in each and every mind. Nothing can be hidden from Me. I will not interfere with human thoughts unless invited. I can keep them on a more divine plane when asked. Stay in the sensitive range of My presence. Your heart can ever be renewed.

Only I know when the end of the world will take place. Take no heed in any predictions from earth. My almighty power will continue to hold the universe together until I give the signal. If people would act as if each day were their last, the world would be in better shape. Love should predominate, but unfortunately only few know how to love.

Vice is rampant as the evil one is stepping up measures to deceive My people. Be not fooled by his tactics. Pray without ceasing to withstand his attacks. Good will end up over evil.

Run your race with courage. You will be ready when I give the signal for the great judgment day. For some it will be a great celebration but for others only doom. My elect should send out warnings. Their efforts will be richly blessed.

Those who treasure their faith will store up for themselves great riches. The eye has not seen nor the ear heard of the wonders My power has produced for My righteous. I promise rewards and My promises are always fulfilled. Ponder on these words and continue on your narrow path.

Let Me sustain you forever with My power. Count on it with confidence that your empowerment is keeping you strengthened against the powers of evil. I care for you even more than your earthly father.

You are among My chosen few to hear and understand about My power. Learn when and how to apply it to your everyday living. Succumb not to this world but continue in the faith until I call you home.

I have blessed you richly with many of My favors. Express your gratitude often and praise Me for them. I live within the praises of My people. You lack for nothing spiritually when you daily walk and talk with Me.

Your new heart can take you to great heights in My Kingdom. Daily build on your firm foundation and no earthly tragedy will shake you. You will understand more and more the length, width, depth and height of eternal truths. My revelations are given only to My righteous. I know who will use them rightly to benefit the church.

Pray for a touch of My almighty power to help you forgive yourself of wrong doing and, in turn, forgive others. This forgiveness is a most important trait to possess. Bitterness can be lifted. If left unaided, the bitterness will fester in the soul and cause much bodily damage. Rid yourself of all anger toward any person by praying for them. Prayer can work wonders when you believe in its power as activated from mine. Your effort can bring about positive results.

Your words and example can encourage others in their steadfast faith. I supply the power behind those words when you remain grounded in My truth. My power penetrates into the core of your very existence. Once you have experienced it, nothing else matters. You want more and more for you know in your heart that you can receive more if you keep pure and holy. You are in control when your mind and heart join in one entity.

Keep My cross ever before you and your own cross will be bearable. I never leave or forsake My righteous. I call and you answer. This is the union I desire and the one for which you were created. I will never stop giving out My grace to sustain you. Endure your hardships knowing that I have a crown awaiting you.

My almighty power brings instant transformation to broken lives. The Holy Spirit works at mending the heart to make one whole. He convicts people of their wrong doing.

There are people that only call on Me when they are sick or in trouble. If they would seek Me in the good times, I would be with them in the bad times.

My gifts of grace sustain My righteous. My eye goes to and fro throughout the earth watching over the faithful. I know every motive before it is ever acted upon. My power picks up your intentions like one of your so-called antennas and there is no interference. Nothing can be hidden from Me. Blessed are those who seek and learn truth.

My power controls every human destiny. Since I am everywhere, no plight is unnoticed by Me. The fear of Me is the beginning of wisdom. I magnify souls in their due season.

Total trust is a "must" in order to live righteously. Heaviness can be taken from the soul. An ease of conscience helps everyone health-wise. People can triumph over all their obstacles when they have learned and then have applied all of My principles. It is the slothful ones who let their flesh rule over their spirit. They will not feel the effects of My power.

You will know through whom I work when you observe the fruits of their labor. Examples are all around for those who keep their eyes open. Watch and pray lest you fall. The evil one is constantly feeding you negative thoughts. Succumb not to his tactics. He would like to keep you confused and worried.

You have the power given by Me to make the right decisions, but pray first. Then remember that all things happen for good to those who love Me. This promise may be seen in your world but, if not, your proof will come in My Kingdom. Your satisfaction and happiness there will be beyond your comprehension.

My power will put you on a high pinnacle in life. Only pray and ask for it if you are willing to sacrifice your own life. The world is demanding and cruel. My people are hurting. Your compassionate heart can bring satisfaction to their souls. Only My love and power can keep you in that state of service where you are willing to go the extra mile.

I am capable of transforming lives through My almighty power. Put your loved ones in My hands and show complete trust in Me. People can worry from lack of trust and thus place themselves in the evil one's hands.

Patience is a virtue to be practiced. It teaches many a lesson. Pray continuously to uphold My standards and the grace you need will be given you. When you see actions of others that are displeasing to you, pray about them. Prayers solve more problems than does confronting offenders. Thus, ill feelings toward others can be kept to a minimum.

Once you realize My love, your soul will take on new aspects of peace. I will increase as you decrease. My power will come to you as a mighty wind. You can inhale it into your innermost being. As you act in My stead, it can perform miracles beyond your imagination. Your words said in faith will well up as a spring of living water. Guard your gift well and use it to edify the Church.

Only those whom I trust receive My power for use under My direction. They recognize My promptings and carry them through. All things can become possible to those who truly believe. Ask for My power and I will release it as I see fit for your needs and the needs of those you wish to help. It takes added strength to minister to My people. A ministry is draining but rewarding.

I am an omnipotent God. I will not withhold My gifts from My faithful servants. I back each one with My power,

but first I must have your complete trust. When negative
thoughts arise, you must cast them out in the name of My
Son, Jesus. Evil lurks around and attacks the minds of those
who do nothing to stop the invasion. Learn about your rights
and privileges from My word. You can find out how to live
victoriously.

*My presence must be felt at all times. Your joy will reveal it to oth-
ers. It can become contagious and My love will spread wherever you
travel. I am counting on you to take an active part in these latter
days of the great harvest.*

The instrumentality of My divine power is orchestrated
throughout the earth. By keeping your mind on Me, you will
see and hear with your spiritual eyes and ears and understand
the vastness of the universe with the spiritual wars occurring.
Only prayers can push away the darkness, along with quoting
My word. Thus harmony is brought about and contentment
automatically follows. This all results from acting upon spiritual understanding. Remember, you are in the world but not
of the world.

*Do not let people get you down. The world's remarks should not
phase you. Rise above and live in My higher plane. You will be
equipping yourself for My gifts, which are many. My love which I
can give you freely will cause you to love your enemies. You can walk
securely in My footsteps. Taste and see what I have to offer. It will
keep you from turning back to the old life. All things become new.*

I am working, even when you experience a dry period, carrying you to a higher plateau. When there are interruptions of
little ones, I understand because I have placed them in your
charge. The same goes for helping the old and the sick. Just
rest in Me and I will give you the patience and endurance to
withstand your trials. I do not expect the impossible. I know
everything that you are going through. You are gaining riches
in the hereafter in accordance with the way that you accept
your trials.

Quench not My Spirit and power will be given unto you. Only My power can give you an effective ministry. In these latter days I am pouring out My Spirit upon all flesh. Those who listen and commit themselves to Me will receive the hope of eternal life. No earthly hope lasts.

Set your sights above and I will unfold a new life for you. Your mind can be changed in the twinkling of an eye. Do not look back at the past but begin anew in the present. Your light will shine brighter as you walk in My path of righteousness. The old nature is shed as the new nature develops.

Sin no longer reigns in your life. A new freedom is yours. Accept it as a gift from Me to you. Be grateful that I have found favor with you. Many are not given the opportunities of hearing as you have or the understanding to comprehend with your mind.

Appreciate your gifts from Me and use them for My glory. If you do not hold back, I will not withhold revelations from you. Be ever ready for new secrets by staying in My presence at all times. You will be led to heights unknown.

Let nothing jeopardize your progress with Me. Walk hand in hand with Me and you will not taste death. Your crossover will be one of great jubilation. Rise and shine, for My almighty power and glory are upon you.

Chapter 2
Creative Power

My creative power is added to your numerous gifts. Your creativity can surpass human abilities. New ideas are being given constantly to My righteous. Try them out and look not at them as something unnatural. Your new insights should encourage you to keep close to Me for constant growth. Be always willing to grow spiritually and I will take care of the increase.

I delight in your enthusiasm. Your childlike attitude will bring you excitement throughout your entire life. Some people put on a spiritual show for others but I always know what is in the heart. I do not spare my grace from My righteous. They are winners in My spiritual world. The things I have waiting for them are beyond the human imagination.

Never become discouraged over present situations. They will pass in but a season. Patience is a virtue that will sustain you all through life. Do not stop practicing it.

Your vocation is one I picked out for you. Stay true to it. The road may be rough at times but your accumulation of My grace will far surpass the inconveniences which you experience.

Example brings far more souls to Me than you realize. It is only the fools who make fun of spirituality. Their days are numbered and doom faces them.

Pray for those whom I place in your remembrance. Your pleading prayers touch My mercy seat. New hearts are given out by Me continuously. I am a merciful God and answer My faithful ones' prayers.

Reach beyond your limits for My name's sake and you will have no limitations. Only goodness and kindness avail you.

If you want creative power, try new ideas out but seal each idea with a prayer. It brings about new insights beyond your human imagination. Always seek Me in everything you do and I will bring about what is best for you. You may not see it in your natural realm but trust Me.

A fervent prayer from a righteous person avails much. Righteousness leads to a just life, putting all the virtues into practice. This brings a clear conscience into active play. Nerves subside and rest. Just knowing that you are doing My will is a great tranquilizer. The mind is free for more creativity.

Be still and you will feel My action in and around you. The world should not be your excitement. I fill the niches of your longings. Spend more and more time communicating with Me. Your gifts will be insurmountable. Your heart is ever being changed into My image. You will know without a doubt that I am at work in you. Your peace gives you an ecstasy which you thought unobtainable in your world — all this accomplished through our companionship.

Keep holy so as not to lose the spiritual gifts I have afforded you. Your glorification can continually be earned upon earth. Not many are willing to live in total subjection to Me. But the benefits far outweigh your sacrifices.

Only believe and you will receive. Walk the narrow path and only goodness will follow you. I am the way, the only way. I am the truth, the only truth. And I am the life, the only life.

Those who live their life for Me will receive eternal life. My touch of eternal power will sustain them. Freely I give to those who freely accept Me. My blessings are as numerous as the stars.

Take deep breaths and breathe My presence into your nostrils. Healing takes place throughout the body as you relax with your mind on Me. The very air you breathe can be purified. I will sanctify your soul as you continually practice My presence.

Be not alarmed when temptation comes upon you. Greater am I in you than he that is in the world. The devil is constantly seeking whom he can devour. He attacks the mind with all kinds of thoughts, but pay him no heed by replacing those thoughts with prayer or repeat My name over and over again and he will flee. Your tool is My word. Use it often.

Your renewed mind contains power to be creative. You will be amazed at your talents. I am now in everything you do. My glory is shown through you — yes, even in your frustrations. Your control is noticed by others. My grace is always sufficient to carry you through.

Your eternal rewards are mounting. Little accomplishments lead to greater ones. They pile up and hold together because of your firm foundation.

Never look back but keep pressing toward your high calling. Live one day at a time, even moment by moment. Let your friendship with Me blossom in those moments. In this way you will leave no vacancy in your mind for the evil one to enter — for he waits for the weak moments. Stay strong and be ever ready to chase him out, along with his negative ideas.

Think health at all times and disease will not take hold. The mind has much to do in maintaining a healthy body.

Learn from one another and pass on your creative thoughts to help others, along with the knowledge with which I have blessed you. My people can prosper when they open up to others. Your gift of discernment will help you discard that which is not of Me.

You can be creative just as long as My power flows through you. My gift of the Holy Spirit dwelling in you makes this all possible. Believe and ask of the Holy Spirit and His gifts will not be withheld from you. The power behind the gifts is the force that gives these gifts a supernatural nature. People cannot produce this force on their own.

Some of My obedient, righteous children are given special gifts even without their asking. I wish them to glorify Me through the use of these gifts. I wait patiently for their development and add or subtract according to their use.

My blessing is upon all that you do in faith. My grace helps to fortify your efforts.

Laziness is not of Me but of the evil one. Contentment cannot be gained without struggle. Happy are those who follow in My ways and keep My statutes. They realize that I will not leave them orphans. I test them with fire but they will not get burned. Their heart will ever grow in love as they travel in My footsteps. Count your sorrows all joy for they lead you through a glorification process.

The more you become like Me, the more of My power has been released to you. You can branch out in a number of directions with unlimited talents. The key is to remain sinless. It is not impossible with My grace which I have poured out freely to you.

My children can never stop growing spiritually when they have the will to be righteous. The world loses its grip on My people as they grow in holiness. Seeing with My eyes gives one new perspective. Through My creative power, you have been given eyes to see, over and beyond what your counterparts see. Offer up thanksgiving for the glimpses that you have been privileged to behold.

Those who are walking the path of holiness should expect spiritual experiences. Ask, and they will be given to you. I will not intrude if you are afraid of them. If you boldly proclaim what I have given to you, more will follow.

I compensate those richly who proclaim My glory. Faith can be built up in others from your witnessing. Listen to My promptings.

With creative power new horizons are opened up for human explorations. There is vast knowledge to be absorbed by the human mind in great depth. Many new discoveries can be made by My praying people. I'm delighted with those who seek knowledge to benefit mankind. Their efforts will lead to great satisfaction.

My most important creative feat is to create new hearts. This changes people into My image to do My work upon the earth. Joy permeates the souls of those who have received new hearts. All things become new to the beholder. Pray to become a recipient of My power and you will walk in divine grace.

Worry not about the signs of the times. You are on the earth but for a season compared to the time you will spend in eternity. Just make all of your moments count toward your eternal destiny. Try out your creative abilities and feel My power behind them.

My power working through you brings stamina to your character. Your faith is built up considerably when you see what you and I can accomplish together. Pride must never enter. Otherwise, you will be left alone and fall.

Learn to recognize the evil one's voice and shut him out. Anything negative comes from him. Rebuke him before he has a chance to take hold of your life. Greater am I in you than he that is in the world. Keep repeating this to get it down in your spirit and fear will play no part in you.

My Son was tempted many times but he overcame all temptations. Learn of Him and walk in His paths. Grace can be given to you in abundance and you can overcome every obstacle. My Son carries your burdens when you submit your life to Him.

❖

I promise you no trouble-free life but I do promise to take you through if you remain righteous. You are then one of My family and I watch over you day and night. I draw you ever closer to Me. So faint not and keep on keeping on. The day I call you home will be a great day of celebration.

❖

Self-control is an attribute which I desire all to develop. Unfortunately, few heed My desires. Those who keep their mind on things above become overcomers. For where the mind is, there the heart is also.

❖

Serve My people when time permits but do not neglect your own duties to do so. Ask to be enlightened on how you can please Me. Often, I just want you to pass along love within your own family. Loving people is My greatest commandment. In so doing I can increase that capacity within your heart.

❖

The power given you can be multiplied according to its use. I am in control of the amount I want each person to receive. Question not the motives on why I hold back My power. I am an All-Knowing God and My Will will be done.

❖

Let creativity become alive in you. Try your hand on numerous projects. Then, with your prayer and My help, you can discover a new person within.

❖

Illness can be conquered if you work on the positive. Think wellness, speak wellness and live wellness. I desire you well but you must discard the habit of worry.

❖

Learn to laugh even though things look bleak. New cells in the body are constantly being formed to replace the diseased cells. Fighting with a renewed mind can do much toward gaining your strength back. Then rest often in My love for I love you more than you can imagine.

I know how the evil one attacks the mind. Do not give him occupancy. Chase him out in My name and quote My word. He will soon flee when he sees that you mean business.

Read only lifting material and be careful what you set before your eyes. You must learn how to live while you are living. No one can accomplish this for you.

Endorse yourself for your achievements and thank Me for My help in them. It is our doing things together that makes all things possible.

By being creative you are working with your Creator. Our time together brings results and gains for you everlasting glory. Your spirit rises above the obstacles that hold you down. The spirit gives life. With life you walk in the light. Darkness has no dominion over you.

Hold fast to My word so that your entire being becomes saturated. You will think as I think and creative thoughts will come naturally. My power will bring positive results far beyond your imagination.

Your life need not be dull as the years fly by. I cause things to happen in your favor and for your own good. You may not comprehend My motives but they are in your best interest. My righteous people are never left unaided.

It is My intent for you to become a more perfect gem and I must chip away from time to time to achieve My expectations. When trials come, embrace them gladly, knowing I am at work in you.

Let your mind drift to others and selfishness can be lifted. By thinking positive thoughts and praying for those I bring to your mind, you can stay active and your health will thrive. It is the lazy people who lose out on My blessings.

Be true to My cause and I will stay by your side, guiding you along life's journey. My power will be available to you when you need it — only ask. You will be astounded at the ways I answer.

I will comfort you from My merciful heart when you think that your trials are too hard to bear. I will not give you more than you can stand. My everlasting love abides with you always. No human heart contains My love. Ponder on the vastness of it. As long as you remain in My will, I will never forsake you.

Set new goals for yourself and I will help you meet them. Nothing is impossible when you let Me take complete control of your life. Your trust brings things into being.

Worry enters not when your trust is operating. Have confidence in all that you say or do. Your mind will stay in the positive zone.

Our friendship continually increases as you practice My presence. You have control of the reins of our friendship.

Because of their sin and lack of acknowledgment, I leave My children to shift for themselves. They will inevitably fall but their cry for help and forgiveness will bring My return.

Be good stewards with your possessions. To those who have been given much, much is required by Me.

Sing songs of praise in your heart. Include your blessings in your thanksgiving. You will be amazed how you can keep your spirit lifted.

It is important to bring your mind and heart into one entity. Speak from the heart and your mind will follow suit. It takes effort on your part to put into practice My teachings. Creativity is born out of your determination to succeed.

Keep Me in the center of your activities. I put into play thoughts that have been stored in the mind. The release of these thoughts will open up new horizons. Spend time in prayer over them.

Try new endeavors and see how I work with you on them. You will be amazed at what we accomplish together. By staying in My will your abilities become boundless.

I will give rest to your soul. Take time often to listen to Me. The body machinery must shut down at times for new cells to form and take over. I help in this process when you continue in My will.

Think on the positive side of every situation. Your spirit will remain in an up-swing mood. Your control of "self" is of vital importance.

Let your overflow of energy spill on your neighbors and friends. Your love shown will witness much for their observance.

Be merciful and compassionate and you will be walking in My footsteps, I in you and you in Me. With much practice you can learn to live victoriously.

The gravitation of the world constantly pulls you away from Me. When you truly understand this fact, you can rise above all its temptations.

I create new power in you to sustain your needs. This power helps you to see beyond your own years. Your understanding is sharpened and new opportunities can surface. Only believe and you will receive.

It is hard for the human mind to fathom the things that occur in the spiritual world. I make it possible for some of My people to see through their spiritual eyes and reveal a small amount of truths to them. For most people it is like seeing through a glass darkly.

You must have faith to believe what seems impossible. Remember with Me all things are possible. My creative power makes it so.

My righteous people are in Me, and I in them, so creative ability will surface. My power will back the things I want revealed to My people. Be not afraid to let the world know what My Spirit conveys.

⸻

The time is crucial to take My messages to the world. People are more vulnerable now to grab onto eternal facts. They see the wickedness in the world as never before. Be a part to turn this around through your own example. Ask Me for a position to handle that will best suit your state in life. Your willingness will bring about an answer.

⸻

Your prayer life must be a steady one. Ever increase your time with Me and I will help you accomplish what you set out to do.

⸻

I am always ready to create new ideas in your mind to make your life more interesting. It also helps you to keep your mind off "self" for "self" is your worst enemy. Having your mind on things above keeps it elevated. The world loses its hold on you, thus making you sinless.

⸻

You are in Me and I am in you. Whatever you do, do for Me. Hesitate not to spread My word. It will lead you to your eternal destiny. Your rewards will be unlimited.

⸻

Fill your mind with inspired writings and listen to My anointed ones. The world's values will not lead you astray when your mind is staid on Me.

⸻

Commit yourself daily to Me to reinforce your good intentions. I will not withhold My power to work through you for My purpose.

⸻

Those who believe in the Eucharist should receive Me often. I am medicine to their body and soul.

⸻

Keep Me in the Center of all that you do. You will see results in My due season. Give thanks, worship, and praise and I will honor you beyond measure. If you could see what I have in store for My righteous, you would never give up hope in spite of all your setbacks. Those who faint not become great conquerors. My Spirit dwells in them richly.

Help all those that you meet to come to the reality of My undying love. Tell them I desire all to be saved.

Show kindness to the unloved. They are desperate for affection. Keep a smile on your face and you will capture hearts. I expect My friends to win friends for My Kingdom.

Be aware of your faults and work on them so I can bring you to perfection. Never give up or My power will not be available to you. Keep asking Me for your needs. I am listening. When you ask Me for power, I will not withhold it. My children prosper because of My power and grace. All things become possible for them.

First, I create in My children a new heart. Then My love is in them, unless they turn from Me. I will not force Myself on anyone. One's free will holds the reins.

Continue to aspire and you will find satisfaction and contentment. Daily take up your cross with love, knowing it will lead to your crown. Our love lifts the burden of worldly cares.

Listen for My still small voice. It is possible to carry on a two-way conversation. After our encounters you will feel rested. I do not condemn you. If you hear condemnation, it is from the evil one.

My power will carry you through each task that you undertake in My name. Always seal it with a prayer.

I am All in All. In looking back over your life you can see My workings and why I did not grant all of your requests.

Drawing closer to Me should be your aim. My watchful eye searches your heart and soul. Nothing can be hidden from Me. Rely on Me with a trusting heart. I will help carry your burdens. Do not worry.

I want joy to overflow from you into others. This is possible when you keep a smile on your face.

Use your mind for creative purposes and I will give you ideas to expand. Believe and you will receive. Faith is the answer.

Chapter 3
Healing Power

My healing power will flow through you if you will believe and accept it. My hurting people must relax in My love with total dependency upon Me. Power can be transmitted through My faithful ones. Accept being prayed over by My gifted people. My healing power flows freely into those I choose. This power can rejuvenate your body and soul. Yes, the soul needs refurbishing as well as the body. It is My desire to heal both, but most importantly the soul.

Refuse not to be prayed over. Accept My blessings through every means possible. Do not consider praying and laying hands on one another useless. My healing power flows through My special human instruments.

Be open to all My gifts. There is power behind them. My church has survived through the centuries because of My power given freely to My people.

The prayers of My righteous can heal the sick. There is power flowing through prayer. If you have been asked to pray for people, do so with a feeling of spiritual obligation. Your own power will increase as you fulfill your requests. A sense of worth will creep into your being, especially when you hear that your prayers were answered. Your prayers are never wasted. They accomplish great strides in the souls of the recipients.

Become a prayer warrior and your priorities will change

for your own good. The increase of power which you obtain from your prayers can benefit many. The evil one will tell you that praying is a waste of time but that is far from the truth. Praying continually will chase him away. You receive healing in the process.

My anointing is available to My prayer warriors. It contains My healing power. Zero in on My frequency for becoming an effective minister.

All power is given to you from the Holy Spirit within you. He teaches, guides, protects, and ministers to you. He is the gift I promised My apostles just before My Ascension. On the day of Pentecost they received the Holy Spirit and power was given them to heal, along with the other believers in that upper room. This same healing power is given to Christians of My choosing. It is to be used to show forth My glory and bring believers into My fold. Do not underestimate this healing power. Believers will benefit.

Pray over others that the power in you may bring about a healing. Many of My healings are spiritual. This type leads you to eternal life. I call a few of My beloved home early in their years. They fill a special position in My Kingdom.

My healing power is given in small doses. I add or subtract as I see fit. It is up to the individual for its effectiveness. One must remain in a prayerful state to receive My power. It takes active growing faith on a firm foundation to be selected as a candidate. My selections are few and on a trial basis to see how this power is handled. A humble spirit is a prime requisite.

In order to keep My power you must stay plugged into the spiritual realm. My word should be in your heart and on your lips. A strong desire to grow into My image must be present along with a compassionate heart.

My ways of healing are diversified. By reading My word you will find this to be true. My people have picked up ways to pray for the sick which I have honored by sending My healing power through them. Some people are healed through the laying on of hands, some by the nearness of My anointed ones, some by the prayers of the faithful assembled for a healing service, and some through a single prayer of great faith.

A little innocent child can pray with belief and I will honor the prayer. I will send healing through those I choose and to those I choose. Believe that all things are possible and do not waiver. I heal through words, through sacrifices, through deeds, etc. The ways are limitless.

My glory is manifested through healing and brings many souls of the spectators to righteousness, along with those who hear by word of mouth. My miracles take place today as well as when I walked the earth. I am the same yesterday, today, and forever.

Be ever sensitive to My Spirit in you. Never cease praying for the sick. Great wonders will unfold before you if you faint not. The will to sin no more must ever be present in your life. I take My committed instruments and mold them into My image.

Often times suffering brings a person closer to Me and I will allow it for this purpose. It is your relationship with Me that determines your destiny. So, all in all, your healing may not be in your best interest.

My righteous who remain close to Me and trust Me in every facet of their lives become winners. Their total submission to Me will bring peace and joy to them no matter what happens. My power will be given unto them through My various gifts.

Learning My ways is of utmost importance in developing a ministry. Do not underestimate My goodness and power which I want to pour out upon you. You can carry out great works which My Son started upon the earth. His miracles of healing were numerous.

Keep in prayer and deny yourself for the sake of others. You must decrease as I increase in you.

When I am called upon I give you a new heart and gradually your mind is transformed. Old things become new. You see things in a different light. My light changes everything. Your path will stay lit and you will no longer walk in darkness. You will not be free of troubles for the evil one prowls the earth, but My grace and protection will see you through. Happy is the person who remains steadfast in My laws. Our relationship keeps him in a joyous state.

It is imperative that you build up your faith if you want Me to work through you in a healing ministry. It is the Holy Spirit's power that lifts disease from a body. Become well acquainted with the Holy Spirit within.

I have My reasons for healing. Often I wish to increase a person's faith. There is nothing too small that I will not give My undivided attention. I show forth My glory through all types of healing. I try in various ways to draw people close to Me.

After healings, some people will wait for the sickness to return. I do not like to be tested. I delight in those who give thanks. My Kingdom is close at hand for them. Be thankful for all favors, big as well as small. Those who witness with their lips build up the church.

I single out people who have been struck down by the evil one with afflictions to pray for the conversion of sinners. When I call them home they will be taken up high into the heavens. They will be greeted by a vast number of souls who made it to eternity through the prayers of My afflicted ones. There is much work to be accomplished on the earth and everyone can take a part in saving souls, even those confined to a bed.

The inner spirit can rise to great heights in prayer while the outer man perishes. No matter what type body houses the soul there is beauty in the inner person who is righteous. My tabernacle is within where My Spirit dwells and unites with the inner spirit of a person. This all takes place when people commit their life to Me and ask forgiveness of past sins. They are given My strength to cease from sinning through My grace. These people receive My special company and have learned to recognize My voice within them.

The more you learn about healing and apply it in your own life, the more your health will flourish. My words speak life into the soul and body. Your actions become stabilized in truth. Behold all things become new.

Nature is a fine example. There is beauty for the senses to enjoy. This enjoyment alone keeps the body and mind functionlng in a more normal state. My creation can be enjoyed if you seek it. There is no cost involved. My gifts are free.

Realize the role I play in your life and My presence will be felt at all times. The more that you learn of Me, the easier your life will become. I lift the burdens that weigh you down. I have set you free on higher ground to travel in safety. Believe and it will all come to pass.

When I become first in your life, your healing is close at hand. Your needs are met in My way. It is hard for you to understand My ways. They are so different than your ways.

Let the things of the world grow dim as your spiritual sight becomes magnified. You can be My instrument of healing to others. A word or touch does wonders for a point of contact. You can be a seed planter and I will supply the fertilizer for growth.

The closer you draw to me, the greater faith you will possess. With this faith comes power.

My word must be ingested daily to grow spiritually. A repetition of My words keeps the soul in contact with the spiritual realm. Remember that you are in the world but not of the world. When the mind focuses on worldly things it is a deterrent to our friendship.

Our conversations bring healing in both body and soul. You are spiritually anointed by Me personally.

Do not become anxious about your servitude. Often your ideas for serving are not mine. Be patient and love everyone. Your heart must be clear of all malice. If you have trouble with relationships, pray for those who bother you and watch how I change the situation.

Only complete love can bring you to the height of being used as My vessel. Then My power will flow through you as My will chooses. Only a small percentage will be totally healed to show forth My glory. But all you pray over will receive My special blessing.

Healing was not meant for all. Some would forget the real Healer and in time stand the chance of losing their soul. With others, their time has been completed and I want them united with Me. So, do not be disheartened if results are not made known to you. Just keep on keeping on, serving Me.

My gifts are free. Simply ask and I will not withhold them from you. Believe in My mercy and goodness. The gratitude in your heart is My recompense. I consider your praises a bonus. Your desire to take Me as your dearest friend will bring untold blessings. Your love for others will increase as you grow more into My image.

Be of good courage as you travel life's journey. You will experience rough times but I will be your helper. Your trust in Me will see you through. Take each day and enjoy it to the fullest. Set not high standards before you.

The sick should keep hope in their heart. They are to remember that I am a God of miracles. I work on the soul which is the most important. Oftentimes bodily healings are manifested as the soul takes on immortality.

Never underestimate the results of My power. Your mountains of trouble can be reduced to molehills just through a change of heart.

Be open to changes. I give new life and open up new avenues for My faithful to travel. They respond with thanksgiving and praise.

No problem is too big that we cannot solve together. A gradual healing can take place through right attitude and obedience to My laws. My help brings satisfaction to the soul.

Know that I am with you through all of your heartaches and disappointments. You are being molded into My image. My power working in you and through you performs great works, often unknown to you and the recipients. Pray for an increase of this power. It will sustain you throughout your life, along with My grace.

Live in hope of a healing for your body. Your soul is receiving a healing as you live your life for Me. Speak of My goodness and mercy to others. Pray with great devoutness.

Your endurance is drawing you closer to My Sacred Heart. I remove fear, bitterness, hatred, jealousy, and all the human qualities that are not of Me. This is My healing of the soul.

Be thankful that you are experiencing My healing power. You will know without a doubt the change that has been taking place in your inner being.

The Holy Spirit dwells in My faithful to heal, guide, comfort, and even convict you of wrong doing. It is His power that is released from your body when you pray on others. The laying on of hands often transmits power as your hands become an extension of Mine. Do not underestimate what I can do through you when you believe.

Your perseverance and endurance bring you closer to Me as afflictions brought on by the evil one can be turned around for your own good. You can be a witness of My glory.

My light shines through My faithful. Their works become great in My sight. Ponder on My blessings, counting them one by one. The earth will grow dim as My glory engulfs you and shines through you.

Greet all My people with the love I have instilled into you. Your friends will be many. My power and grace in you will sustain you now and forever.

Stress is the biggest deterrent taking the body off nature's course. It instigates many illnesses. Turn your mind on Me and relax your muscles. This can happen in meditative prayer. The evil one flees when you stay in the spiritual realm. My scripture on your lips keeps him from gaining entrance into your mind or body.

Learn of Me and My ways to fight off sickness. You will be aware of My tools and their availability. Become a prayer warrior and intercede for others. What you give to others will come back to you multiplied. My healing power will not be held back in your behalf. When you lay hands on others in faith, they will be blessed by My power flowing through you. You can become My instrument of great price.

People who love others draw My healing power more readily into their being. They are following My greatest commandment. Their ease of conscience brings rest to the soul. When an illness strikes, they have the stamina to see it through, often drawing My healing power which I give out freely to My followers. They can become conquerors. Whatever they face, they keep a positive attitude. No one can take their joy, embedded deeply within their being, from them. Our relationship becomes an ongoing adventure.

Age is not a drawback to constant growth in spirituality. I will favor the elders by putting new ideas into their minds to keep them active. Loneliness will not enter their tent. I will call them by name and they will recognize My call.

　　　　　　　　　　　　　　　〰

Those who have not experienced My voice should not give up but press on toward their high calling. Your perseverance will be rewarded.

　　　　　　　　　　　　　　　〰

My healings last. They are a gift to the beholder. Some cannot fathom My goodness and do not believe their healing came from Me. Their witness is withheld and no glory is given Me. While others believe in My mercy and their thanksgiving is forever on their lips. They become My goodwill ambassadors and touch the lives of many.

　　　　　　　　　　　　　　　〰

Be cognizant of the spiritual protection available to you. Fear will leave and peace can be yours. Just believe.

　　　　　　　　　　　　　　　〰

Healing need not be apparent to the naked eye. If you believe what you cannot see, your faith will grow by leaps and bounds. That type of faith will become honored in ways you cannot fathom, sometimes in your world and sometimes in the next.

　　　　　　　　　　　　　　　〰

Be happy that you have been given the key of understanding. Work diligently at obtaining a high place in My Kingdom. By showing love to My people, I reciprocate with My love flowing toward you. Your insight can be sharpened beyond your imagination.

　　　　　　　　　　　　　　　〰

Keep asking for My gifts with a contrite and humble heart and you will receive what is most suited for your spiritual growth. Your steps will be made light for you have already been lifted.

　　　　　　　　　　　　　　　〰

Give thanks and praise for My goodness shown you. No matter what outcome may befall you, My presence will always bring you hope. Hope brings peace to all My followers.

Your needs are met when you have My peace because peace is everyone's greatest need. Most sicknesses would not take hold if this peace were present in My people. Strive for peace among all people. If nations would do this, wars would cease.

Chapter 4
Power In The Blood

In the Old Testament animal blood was splashed on altars and people, signifying the atonement for sins. The animal was then sent up as a burnt sacrifice to Me. My Son's death upon the cross did away with this custom. His sacrifice on the cross and shed blood redeemed mankind of their sins. They were set free and forgiven. When My people understand this, a new life unfolds before them. They want to follow My commandments and walk in My Son's image.

By accepting My Son as their personal Savior, My people become candidates for My grace and blessings. Their body becomes a tabernacle for the Holy Spirit who will teach and guide them into all truths.

Plead My Son's blood upon anything or anyone you wish. It has great power.

Do not underestimate My power in the Eucharist. I consecrate earth's bread and wine into My body and blood through the priests. They have My anointing power for this most sacred act. If you truly believe when you receive, My strengthening power will flow through you.

My blood will purify your blood and strengthen your heart. You must ask and believe. This puts into motion the intent of the communion ceremony. The last supper was a ceremony to be enacted down through the ages in remembrance of Me.

Great benefits are derived by the people when they seek Me with all their hearts. Preparation must be made with total submission to My will. A reverence must be shown to Me and the onlookers. This is a sacred ceremony and My faithful should feel honored to be able to partake of it.

Ignoring My invitation is a grave mistake and will lead you away from My blessings. Acceptance with understanding will bring My righteous nearer to Me.

You are a special creation and are being blessed for every act performed in My homage. You are indeed fortunate and privileged to partake of My sacrifice. Let your mind dwell often on your spiritual riches. My power will flow through your veins when needed.

Little by little you are being transformed into My image. The doubters do not receive My rich blessings. Happy are they who walk in My ways. My Kingdom is being prepared for their arrival.

For protection from the enemy you can cover people, yourself, and things with the blood of the Lamb. All things said from your lips are heard by Me. Believe with faith,and protection will be yours for there is power in the blood. Fix your eyes on things above and the vexations of earth will not engulf your mind.

The mind is free to dwell on any matters which your will chooses. Sort out the things of value that lead to salvation and think upon them. Plead the blood against the forces that would have you think contrary to My will.

Glory can come upon you in this life and continue in the next. My righteous are washed in the blood of the Lamb. They receive power within and will triumph over the earth. If people realized and understood their power, their potential could be unlimited. They would pray in a different manner.

Prayers are answered when the heavenly forces are put into play. It is the knowledge, acquired and backed by belief, that puts into motion the right motives which bring results.

A person's salvation is the most important thing of all. Never give up praying for souls. It is the highest of callings and it will be made known to you on judgment day just how many you saved. A happy jubilation will be observed by many.

After earthly celebrations one can feel empty but that is not the case in the next world. Your elation is continually built upon. So your prayer life on earth adds to your ecstasy in Heaven.

Prepare yourself to receive Me in Communion as you would make preparation for a special visitor. Just as you would sweep your house clean so you must come to My banquet table with a clean soul. Come with a thankful heart and My mercy will be upon you. The power in My blood will help you to live in a more productive manner and give you the courage to finish your course in life. My blessings will be poured out upon those who receive Me in a rightful manner. Learn the meaning of the great privilege set before you.

My blood was shed for the remission of sins. What great power it embodies. Cover yourself and others with it, always using it with reverence and praying in My name. The results will be felt by you and bring you peace. Evil runs from it. I give My followers the authority to plead My blood. Their faith brings it into their possession. They are blessed beyond measure with its use. Consider yourself indeed fortunate.

My people must show to others their faith and their trust in order to draw them into My fold. Action on your part will bring results. Faith without actions is dead.

Dare to grow in the Spirit. A higher place in the next world will be awaiting you. Use the tools available to you and especially keep in

*mind the power in the blood — not animal blood, not human blood,
but the blood of the Lamb, Jesus. This divine blood will perform wonders when I pour it forth on the hands of My servants. Their anointing will accomplish My purpose.*

You have triumphed over sin and death because you have
been washed in the blood of the Lamb. The spiritual aspects
that continue in the spiritual realm are mind boggling. You
need not dwell on analyzing them. Believe through faith and
you will thrive on My gifts. Ask in faith and you will find out
for yourself My laws of reciprocity.

*Remember, I know what is best for your well-being. Accept each
gift in humble submission to Me. I am the craftsman of your new
heart, molding you more and more into My image.*

I will be supportive of any ministry which you take upon
yourself to spread the gospel. What you think of as limitations will be no hindrance with My help. Form a bond with
Me and our union can accomplish great works in your world.

*The mind can be expanded. Cover it with the blood of the Lamb
each day by the words of your mouth. The evil one cannot cross the
blood line. There are many thoughts put upon the mind by the evil
one and, when dwelt upon, they become unhealthy and even sinful.
Every precaution must be taken to avoid these thoughts and the will
must be trained to cast them out.*

Magnify Me, for I am the Almighty, Powerful God. My
power is given out to those I choose, and in small doses. It is
electrifying. A human being can take just so much to remain
standing. It is given out to honor and glorify Me on certain
occasions. It is also given for protection from evil forces when
asked for from the lips of a believer.

*There are many ways to grow in My image. Latch onto as many
as your human heart can conceive. You are rich beyond measure with
your growing faith. It is priceless when you speak in terms of value.*

All that you have is a gift from above and the greatest is the gift of faith. Through faith comes power. This power makes all things possible.

Meditate on My Son's death. No one can fathom the ignominious death that He endured. The blood which He shed was for all people to save them from sin and death, thus signifying the power in the blood. All mankind has to do is acknowledge Jesus as their Lord and Savior. The price that He paid was beyond human endurance.

Our freedom was bought for that price. Thanksgiving should be forever from the heart to your Savior. Establish a close relationship with Jesus and Me, your God. Discuss everything with us and plead the blood upon it. Your conversation will thus become a prayer.

Those who follow My commandments receive the Holy Spirit to dwell within, to lead and guide them. My people become rich in My grace when they follow the path I set before them. It is those who rebel that lose out on all I have to offer.

Be of good courage to show your faith and spread it around. Your efforts will reap a harvest which often comes from small seeds which you plant. Your good example does wonders for the onlookers. My peace will follow you even in the midst of your storms.

Those who believe that power is given to them through the shed blood can become worry free. Their habit of pleading the blood becomes a prayer of protection. Praying in such a manner for their loved ones brings a secure feeling to the one who prays in true faith.

Becoming knowledgeable about the spiritual realm and your rights can prevent sicknesses. It takes a firm commitment on your part to keep from sinning and walk in the path of righteousness. When the evil one realizes your strong stance against him, he flees. But be on guard for his return and use the sword of the spirit, My word. Scriptures memorized and repeated out of your mouth push the enemy away. My words do not come back to Me void. They will always accomplish My purpose.

I shed My blood at the pillar for your sicknesses and diseases. If you believe this, the power in My blood can erase some of the symptoms the evil one tries to put upon you. You were set free and do not have to listen to his deceptions. Meditate on My scourging and plead the blood I shed to cover hurts. There is still power in that blood today.

Learning to live in the spiritual realm can do much for your welfare. Be not afraid to pass your learning on to others. They may laugh at you but they will remember and act when they hurt and thus prevent an illness before it captivates their body.

Making your life a continual prayer is a beneficial asset that no one can take from you. I release My power in mighty ways to help My righteous people who believe. Doubters miss out on My numerous blessings. Pray to become a positive person and ask that the negativism be removed.

Some prayers are answered slowly but in the process you can grow in patience. This is a great virtue that will keep you out of much trouble. Your happiness depends on its development.

Judge not My people. I deal with each one differently. What may be a sin for one is not for another according to each one's circumstance. The rules that some abide by may not fit you.

Draw close to Me and let Me be your teacher. Forget not the power of My shed blood. Imitate the love that I have for a My people. Do good for others in spite of the treatment that you receive in return. In this manner you are planting seed that is not left unnoticed.

You can become an earthen vessel and a likely candidate for My power. Miracles are performed each day through those of My choosing. I am the same yesterday, today, and forever.

Be not afraid of your potential when My power flows through your veins. Be willing to be used and you will not regret it. Receiving a mixture of the spiritual realm adds excitement to your life. But, denying the possibility of receiving power from My blood eradicates the power intended for you.

Speaking out My words from scripture gives life to them and My power becomes yours as your faith grows. You are rich beyond measure when you believe the great truths found in My word.

My power flows through you freely when you have been given the Holy Spirit to dwell within. Your understanding is sharpened as He teaches your mind. Your heart and mind can become one entity. My grace heaped upon you along with My power brings possibilities to the surface that you never dreamed could be available for you.

My blood can flow through your veins to give you new health and vitality. Just ask. Keep yourself pure and holy to obtain the gifts which I have to offer. My spiritual world will become alive to you and shut out the lies that your world uses for allurements. Only I can satisfy the soul and make it whole.

A transfusion of My blood can revitalize your immune system. The requisite is to ask for it in faith. Believe that you have received and apply My words to seal our pact. Do not let symptoms which you feel affect your belief. I put My people through many tests for their own benefit. Do not give up for you may be just a hair away from your miracle.

Hope in the heart can keep one on top of all his or her problems. Be grateful for what you have and sing songs of praise to Me.

Never be envious. You do not know all the circumstances of anyone's life or what one will go through down life's journey. Judge not and you will not be judged.

Seek Me in every situation and you will have My blessings. The nearer you draw to Me, the nearer I draw to you. Our love relationship grows until we become one. My blood mixes with your blood and flows through you with power. Plead for it, especially when fearful occasions arise and protection is needed. I dwell in My faithful ones and they learn to live life more abundantly.

I expect My people to share their beliefs with others. Your witness will be effective only if your life shows forth My love. Example is the chief tool for conversions.

The Holy Spirit empowers you and takes you to higher plateaus as you grow in holiness. Making your life a continual prayer brings My Spirit's assistance when needed. The fruits of the Spirit radiate in My faithful ones. They are love, joy, peace patience, long suffering, gentleness, kindness and endurance.

Possession of these fruits automatically connects you to the spiritual realm. Everything becomes possible. Plead My blood as a safeguard against the enemy.

Your family can benefit greatly by your acting upon your new-found beliefs. Discover for yourself your direct line of communication with Me.

Let Me increase as you decrease. Your world will grow dim with My sight. Your spiritual eyes and ears become attuned to My calling. Your longings become of a supreme nature. The soul becomes satisfied when higher powers are put into play.

My words carried in your heart will be spoken from your lips automatically. They become strength to your mortal flesh. Waste no time with worldly adventures but feed upon My word and, in turn, feed it to My people. Power is given to you when you live in the Spirit.

⟶

Continually cover yourself with My blood each day by reciting it from your mouth. Power will flow through you when My work becomes top priority.

⟶

Your love for Me must be genuine. Doors will be opened up to you that you never thought possible. A training period is required but you can pass the test. Fear will leave as you experience My power.

⟶

When you drink from the chalice and truly believe that you are drinking My blood, your blood is being strengthened and the chalice where you touch your lips is purified. Belief sanctifies all of your actions, for My power is at work in My believers. Grace is added to grace. There are no limits to My outpouring. We become one as I and My Father are one.

⟶

Continue to receive My Body and Blood as much as possible and speak to Me at great lengths. I know your needs but want to hear them from your lips. Praise Me for I dwell in your praises. Keep yourself pure and undefiled. I will reveal myself to you in unprecedented ways.

⟶

Seek always the better things in life and they will be added unto you. Your glory can start in your world and continue on into the next. My storehouse is full of wonderful surprises awaiting you. Mull this over in your mind when your spirit reaches a low level.

⟶

Negative thoughts must be erased for My words to become effective. I am gentle and loving and have no intention of dealing with My righteous harshly. Your sins are forgiven and forgotten after you have confessed them to Me with a contrite heart. Just sin no more and work on your perfection.

⟶

Trust in Me for all your needs. Pray for My grace to sustain you. Living a righteous life keeps you tapped into My power. The holy Spirit is the source.

An added source is through My blood. Learn to proclaim it. Its powers are unlimited for a believer. Cover yourself and loved ones each day for protection. A simple statement to use is: I cover (myself or name of person) with the blood of the Lamb. The enemy recognizes this coverage and flees.

Keep My statutes and hold firm to My promises and you will have the light of life. Your race can be run in dignity. Use the tools I have provided to help you run your race. Peace will flood into your soul. This peace has no price for it cannot be bought. It is only obtained through Me.

Your faith is strengthened day by day when you live for Me. Think of ways to spread My love and follow through with action. Forget not to seal these actions with My blood. They then become divine and take on true meaning.

You can rise to great heights in your world when you ask Me to be in your thoughts, words and actions. The evil one will try to tell you that your good deeds are useless and you may experience feelings of hopelessness. When you stumble and fall under human weakness, pick yourself up by asking for My strength. Trials in life will befall you but do not hesitate to ask My forgiveness. Keep your eyes on My cross and take up yours each day to venerate Me. You will then have no regrets to ponder upon in your latter years.

Your role in life is to be My servant by serving others. Thus your love, as an extension of My love, will shine through. My power from on high is within you, especially when you plead My blood. It covers a multitude of purposes, unknown to the secular mind but available to My servants for greater use.

Be bold in professing the good news of the gospel. I will give you the right words needed when you stay close to Me in prayer. That is one of many gifts the Holy Spirit provides.

Pray always to the Holy Spirit for guidance in use of the power entrusted to you. Your belief makes all things possible. Many people do not make use of the power endued them. Their potential in the spiritual realm is not achieved. Often fear holds one back. Cover yourself with My blood through the words of your mouth and the evil one will flee along with the fear.

Fear keeps one bound. I came to loose the bonds that keep one captive. Fear is not from Me. I give love, power, and a sound mind. Repeat this last sentence over and over again. The mind needs to be fed by repetition of My words and prayer will unite the mind and heart as one entity.

Coordinate your thoughts with Mine. Let not the world's thoughts occupy your mind. You are your mind's only keeper. Cover your mind each day with the blood for the evil one cannot cross the blood line. This principle may seem strange as repeated a number of times in this chapter but you will find it works and will give you great satisfaction and consolation. Your family members and friends can benefit greatly if you cover them, not only on special occasions, but daily as they walk their journey in life.

Selfish people do not pray for others but My prayer warriors have overcome selfishness. They have learned how to live by My principles. Blessed are they for I do not hold back My grace from them.

Form the habit of praying for people in the market place. Your shopping will not become a drudgery. Your time spent in line will pass fast and will not be wasted. Life takes on new meaning when prayer becomes the focus of your attention.

Distractions will occur in prayer but erase them from your mind and learn to develop better and longer attention spans. Ask for help and I will not withhold ways to counteract you weaknesses.

Joy cannot help but creep into the souls of My righteous. It is evil that eats away at the heart causing continual unhappiness. I replace old hearts with new ones when My people repent of their sins and truly ask forgiveness. They must acknowledge Me as their Lord and Savior. I will sprinkle My blood with theirs and the blood flowing through their veins will be purified.

My death on the cross and rising should prove to mankind the truth of My revelations. I conquered death for all of mankind. But only those who believe, repent of their sins, and are baptized will be saved.

The Bible reveals My true identity. I expect My people to pick up their cross daily and follow Me. My shed blood contained the power to redeem the world. No power on earth can save. You can rise again in eternal life. Do not jeopardize your chances by giving in to earth's allurements.

Picture yourself rising in your new white garment of righteousness. There is one reserved just for you without spot or wrinkle.

Ponder on My words and see for yourself how they will come to pass. A few of My saints have received their glorification on earth but most of My righteous receive a little on earth and continue their glorification in eternity.

There is life in the blood. Use it to live more abundantly. It is not a silly gesture to cover people and objects with My blood. When you grow more in My image, you speak life in your words.

Believing in your power is hard for My faithful ones to comprehend. It takes much trust with a daily building of faith on a firm foundation to keep from wavering. I reveal myself in many ways to confirm your convictions.

Be mobile to spread the good news that has been revealed to you. Added enlightenment will be given to you in the magnitude that you reach out to others. Your faith will never stop growing. Your mind

*can be expanded through spiritual awareness. Never think it too dull
to comprehend My teachings.*

Faith is a gift from Me that your intellectual friends do not
possess. You can even cover your faith with My blood by
speaking it into being. The powers of evil know when your
faith is sealed and will stay away from you.

Chapter 5
Everlasting Power

My everlasting power given you will last forever and ever. Some receive it on earth and carry it with them to their eternal home.

Without power your words would mean nothing. Those who have power in them recognize My words and receive them with gratitude. Life takes on real meaning when My power dwells within My faithful ones. A purpose for living is established and continues until My role call.

Seek the things above and you will not be left behind when My power is given. Learn of Me and My desires will become your desires. We will walk down life's path together and evil will flee because of My presence. Your understanding will become sharpened as you take in My truths. My power opens up the dormant cells of understanding. Pray for more and more of it.

Do not let your mind drift as you are taking in My word. Practice on concentration by casting out all thoughts of distraction in My name. You will surprise yourself at how well this process can work.

You must work toward being perfect if you wish to become one with Me. My saints have followed this practice and they are reaping the harvest.

Do not complain about lack of time. It becomes available when

My will and your will can work in perfect harmony.

The power in you will recognize the right hour to work toward showing forth My glory. There are stop and go signs to follow. For now it is like seeing through a glass darkly but My power can give you gleams of light. The path to follow along life's journey will be shown more clearly as you continue to draw closer to Me.

Worldly things need not draw your attention when spiritual things take precedence. The fascination of the spiritual world can hold your interest until the day I return to take you to your eternal home. My rationed power will keep you content.

The human body cannot contain too much power. You might compare it to electric voltage. Too many currents could not keep one standing. Keep your body in good running condition to withstand more of My power. Rest is essential, along with proper nourishment.

The needs of people are enormous. Pray that you may be given the wisdom and understanding to know what part that you should take to help meet some of their needs.

While you are doing routine chores you can pray and you will find that your time will pass by quickly and yet gain for you satisfaction that you have helped others in the process.

My power adds strength to your weakness. You will discover that you can do so much more than you ever dreamed possible when you call on Me for strength.

It takes much practice to listen to the truths my word implies. Memorize My words and repeat them over and over again until they become a reality. There is power in them to fight off any evil that tries to come against you.

Never neglect to use the name "Jesus". It brings instant help. The name itself contains power. If you repeated the name over and over again, your spirit would grow tremendously.

Love everyone. You have the capacity. Especially work at loving your enemies. All bitterness will cease on your part and you will learn what forgiveness is all about. Unless people develop a forgiving heart, they will not grow in love.

My power is permanent and will never change. I change not. You were rescued from darkness and shown the light. A sense of future security is implanted in your soul, a confidence in your own eternal life.

Consume all the knowledge that you can of the spiritual nature. Retreat to a quiet place to soak it up. Listen for My still small voice. I reveal Myself in many ways to My righteous. They become candidates for My power.

All things are possible when My power is given. Receive it in thanksgiving and do not fear it. I will not force My power on anyone who is reluctant to receive it.

Keep in prayer to remain open to My Spirit. I draw close to those who draw close to Me. Our intimate relationship lifts you to a higher plane to receive some of My glory. Your joy will increase as you climb the spiritual ladder.

Evangelize among the people. I will speak through you. You will not be left alone. Where you gather in My name, I am in the midst. You will find that your timidity is lifted.

My everlasting power stays with My anointed ones and comes in the form of a gift. This type of gift is given to a select few of My choice. They have been molded to handle their important position on earth with humility. I add more of My power from time to time to accomplish My purpose.

Most of My people recognize their gifts and joy floods their soul.

They work diligently to perform their tasks under My anointing.

Those who want My special gifts must give their lives completely over to Me. They must draw close to Me in prayer. Then, in My due season, I will bless them in ways they least expect.

Forming a love relationship with Me will spur you on. I do not promise an easy life, but a fulfilling one.

Too many people waste their time on pleasures. Their lives become empty and their happiness vanishes. Your joy from your relationship with Me will continue growing in your earthly life and last forever and ever.

You can love your enemies through the power I have given you. All bitterness and hurts will vanish. My everlasting power in you makes this possible. Forgiving comes fast and easy when you pray for those you dislike or those who have hurt you. This is My desire for you so that you grow in My image.

The human body stops growing at a certain age but your faith will never stop growing when you seek Me with all your heart. Persevere in prayer and think on Me. You can become My jewel of great price with My polishing.

As long as you live in the world there will be trials, but you can use them as stepping stones toward perfection. The evil one attacks the strongest when one goes through troubles and sicknesses. Let not your weakness affect your faith. My grace will be sufficient to see you through.

Wear a smile to pick up the downtrodden. Let words of faith be on your lips. You can cause a soul to make an about-face from evil.

Good example should be shown at all times. Your light will shine through for all to see. Do not underestimate the good that you can do for My people. My power in you makes things happen.

My glory is revealed through My willing servants. Age or status in life makes no difference. Much can be accomplished by walking step by step to further My Kingdom. I desire your full attention. Your circumstances have allowed you to fulfill My desires. Let not the evil one pull you in other directions. Discipline yourself. You will feel good about your accomplishments and your soul will be satisfied.

Expect changes; they are inevitable. Often they are for your own good. Praise Me for them. I am in the midst of the praises of My people.

You can depend on My everlasting power to take you through good times as well as bad times. You will feel My added strength. My goodness and kindness will follow you all the days of your life. You are a family member of long standing. Your faith has been built on a firm foundation.

Chapter 6
Transmittable Power

Touching is important, that My power may pass from you into others. You can be the instigator of My transmittable power flow.

Unbelievers can become believers for My power creates new hearts. Do not underestimate what My power can do.

Lay hands and pray on one another. You will be acknowledging My presence and some will feel it. I make things happen. For those who laugh and outwardly show disbelief will, nonetheless, have a seed planted in them. I can eventually cause it to grow.

Circumstances happen in life to change people. Your prayers for the lost all help to bring souls to My Kingdom. What a glorious day you will have on your homecoming.

Prayer groups are on the right track when they hold hands and pray. My power is transmitted to all and through all. More faith is given unto you if you doubt not.

Grace upon grace is added for your faith to grow. You become rich spiritually in My eyes. No one who is against you will prosper. You have my guiding light and will see the way clearly for your journey in life.

Ask to be used as My vessel. Then stay in close unity with

Me. I will not let you down. Only joy will flood your soul.

You can pray silently for people in the marketplace. I can transmit My power through your thoughts into the person you wish to receive a blessing.

I can also transmit My power across the country. Distance is no barrier. Your prayer must be genuine and sincere. Your petition may not get answered but a blessing is always given. My timetable is different than yours.

Christian friends become an asset to you. They can help you in your process of learning and pick you up when you are down. Oftentimes I will send people to you to help you in time of need. You can also administer help to them.

People who keep in prayer are greatly blessed. The forces of the world may be tempting but they receive the grace to rise above any evil.

When a situation seems too overpowering for you to handle, call upon a spiritual friend to lay hands upon you and pray with you. Great comfort can come through My faithful ones.

Once you have been given some of My transmittable power, your spirit can pass it on to others. It is a love power. Your compassionate heart wants others to have the joy which you possess. Touching others can pass on this love power.

Mingle among My people and reach out and touch, knowing some of My spirit power in you can plant a seed in others. Let your life show nothing but good example. Your light can shine to brighten someone's world.

Be prepared to answer questions through your knowledge of the scriptures. You can eventually lead people to My word. My wish is that everyone be drawn unto Me. You can become an evangelizer in many ways and your rewards will keep multiplying.

If you intend to speak out in My name at a gathering, pray about it beforehand. I will put power filled words in your mouth that will transmit power to others to open their ears for understanding.

Where groups are gathered in My name, I show forth My glory of the Spirit through certain individuals. Pray to be a recipient. My favor will rest upon you when special occasions arise. You will come to recognize it and act upon it for My name's sake.

By being a carrier of My transmittable power, you can plant seeds in others. Let the Spirit lead you all the way. You will have this feeling deep within that you are carrying out My wishes.

I do not want anyone to perish. You may be the link for someone else in the chain for their salvation. Never underestimate what My power through you can accomplish.

Be willing to be a human sacrifice for others and you will be walking in My footsteps. Using your time to pray for others is worthwhile and pleasing to Me. Your healing can be taking place at the same time.

Pray especially for those who have hurt you. An emotional healing will spring forth and forgiveness will blossom within.

You can accomplish much in the silence of your heart. Only you and I know your heart's intent. Others do not have to know. After all, I am the rewarder.

I am also the judge. Keep away from making judgments. What you see and hear can bring about false accusations. Truth is often hidden.

My ways are true ways. Walk in them and you will stay in My light. It will guide you throughout your earthly journey.

Mortify your flesh and you will walk in the spirit. Fasting

is a good way to keep your flesh under subjection. Your soul can be strengthened when acts of mortification are applied.

Learn to say "no" to the things of the world that have a tendency to pull you down. Your conscience will aspire when you look back. There will be no regrets.

Tell others about My grace and mercy. I will send My power through your words. Some words are anointed to accomplish My will. Pray that the words coming from your mouth have My sanction. What you hear coming out can astound you for I will speak through you.

When there seems to be no way out, I can make a way but you must call on Me with faith in your heart. My answer may not be immediate but be assured that I have your best interest at heart.

Leave your problems in My hands and erase them from your mind. Speaking about them is a hindrance toward My action.

My power flows through My trusting, faithful people. Doubt stops the flow and worry shows a lack of trust.

Continue to strengthen your faith. Synchronize your mind, body, and spirit so that the flesh will not war against the spirit. Fight your battles against the evil one by quoting My scriptures.

Help others by showing forth your spiritual methods. Some do not realize that they can pray for more faith. With a willingness on their part to receive, I will honor their request.

Establish Christian relationships so that temptations will not be so prevalent. You can learn from one another because, in number, there is strength. Where two or more are gathered in My name, there I am in the midst of them.

It is pleasing to Me when you come away with Me in the sanctuary of your heart. Our love relationship can grow rapidly. I will send My transmittable power through you to others with encouraging words and they can benefit from this power. Your love for others will produce seed which I will cultivate.

Never give up praying for your friends and relatives that you deem hopeless. Maybe just one more prayer would help them turn around.

Thank Me for the power that you feel is working through you. With thanksgiving, I will accompany more of the same. You can become an asset to your friends and I will give them that realization.

Blessings upon blessings, and grace upon grace, are given to those who sacrifice for Me. In due season you will come to realize that what I am saying is true.

Be not dismayed by the things happening in your life. My power brings them about to produce much fruit and show forth My glory.

In time, our relationship will be all that you want. I am all-sufficient to meet each one's needs according to My riches. Your riches are looked upon differently by the world. Oh, the glory that you can behold when we are joined together in eternal life! The finite mind cannot comprehend all that I have to offer. So, you have some wonderful surprises awaiting.

You are allowed to daydream about your eternity. It will bring about a calm assurance in your personage. It helps you to fight the good fight for your eternal salvation. Help others to do likewise by speaking out about the goodness that is happening to you inside. I will never stop giving out My power when you utilize it for the good of My people.

Banish all sorrow from your mind. The evil one will always try pressing you back into his corner but power will be given to fight his tactics through My grace. All of your sorrows can be translated into joy as you learn to think the way I do.

Repeat your purpose for living: to know, love, and serve Me so that you can be happy in the next life. All earthly pleasures can fall by the wayside as your interest in Me takes precedence.

Decipher My words in the Bible and dwell upon them. Pray to be enlightened before reading. The power in the word will come forth upon you. I open the senses of those I want to absorb the good news.

My people are unaware of the power I can give them. They must speak with authority in My name to the evil one placing symptoms of illness upon them. They should not accept them as coming from Me. I desire all to be in good health and prosper. Learn of Me and you will not be ignorant.

The mind has much room to expand. I can open up channels with My power given unto you. Pray for enlightenment. You will be amazed at your potential, especially in the spiritual realm.

When you are stumped on a certain problem, ask for My power and I will transmit it quickly to you to help you figure out the right answer.

Constantly, I am opening up new avenues for My people to explore but worldly pleasures choke them out. Noise from electric boxes in the average home snuffs out communication with Me.

A quiet place must be established for retreat where you can bring peace to your troubled heart. A relationship with Me is the answer.

The evil one will try to enter into our rendezvous but you must throw him out using My words which act as your sword of the spirit. Have verses memorized to be prepared for battle. The enemy's negative words cannot take roots in you. Believe only the positive thoughts which are from Me and those roots will grow and blossom.

My people are My lights shining in the darkened world to show others the way. I'm counting on them to bring many into My Kingdom. Pray for My will in the part I want you to play. Your answer will come and be confirmed through others.

Those who do My will please Me greatly. I will not hold back My power but send it through them so they can carry on My work upon earth.

Sin must cease in order to have My Spirit work in you. My saints have all conquered it and so can you. It becomes easy with your new heart. Love for all can saturate your soul.

When you are committed to My will in every aspect of life, My peace will be with you and joy will flood your soul. You need only Me to accomplish this feat.

Self-control has brought you thus far. Too many in the world just think of self. They want to gratify their flesh. My people make an effort to gratify their spirit.

I will implant wisdom in your soul and you will stay on top of your problems. It is more priceless than gold.

I am your good shepherd who leads you beside the still waters. I anoint your head with oil. Goodness and mercy are yours for I dwell within. My mercy is upon you even though you walk through the valleys. Lo, I am with you always and the last day I will take you up to dwell with Me for ever and ever. Think often on these uplifting words.

The evil one throws road-blocks in your way with all his negative ideas which he tries to implant into your mind. Pay him no heed and rejoice that you have been given the eyes and ears of understanding.

―――

I have worked out your salvation. Your sins have been forgiven. You are set free. But sin no more and walk in My righteousness. The tools have all been given you to accomplish My purpose of saving souls, your own as well as many others.

―――

My power will help you when you feel weak. Call for it often. You will be furnished what is needed when you keep in prayer. My children will not lack for spiritual benefits.

―――

Do not let selfishness stand in your way but reach out to friends, neighbors, and even strangers. Balance your life with prayer. You will become enlightened in your ways to go.

―――

Receive My power when it comes and put it to good use for My glory. More will be added when you step out in My name. I am at work in you molding you in My image. Submit yourself entirely to Me.

―――

You cannot fathom My great love for you and it is everlasting. Know that I am with you walking every step of the way. I know all your thoughts so keep them pure and undefiled. Rest in the assuredness of My loving arms about you. Joy will flood your soul in spite of every circumstance.

Chapter 7
Angelic Power

My angels are given power to accomplish My assignments. You have no idea how many times they have been sent to rescue you. You have a guardian angel but often this angel has been reinforced with My warring angels to help battle evil ones who have tried to engulf you .

Converse with your guardian angel. He will appreciate your acknowledgement. The more you practice living in the spiritual world, the holier you can become.

The angels rejoice over every sinner who accepts Me as their Savior. They work diligently to bring people to My Kingdom. They become a part of your conscience voice, prodding you to do good. Listen and do not ignore them. If you receive negative vibrations, it is the evil one at work.

Your guarding angel is someone special. It is proper to give your angel a name. He is a servant of God and sent to watch over you and guide you. Think back at the times that you escaped death or injury. Your special angel was watching out for you and protected you from danger. He pleads on your behalf and prays for you. You are helped in time of trouble. He is an angelic spirit ministering to your needs. Thank him by name. I say him but there is no sex in the spiritual world so the name can be male or female. My warring angels have male names, like Michael, Raphael, Gabriel, etc. Call on them when you feel you are being overwhelmed by evil.

Keep your soul in the state of grace and you will have heavenly bodies working on your behalf. You have no idea what is taking place in the spiritual world. Much is a mystery but I will give you signs of awareness from time to time.

You need not be lonely when your innermost being has many contacts in My world. Rejoice that you have some understanding for I have opened up your spiritual eyes and ears. Many cannot believe like you, but do not force your beliefs upon them. Just plant a seed here and there and keep in prayer for them.

To some people I pour out My grace abundantly. I expect it to be used for My honor and glory. If you are uncertain of the direction to go, stop and pray. I will speak to you through many ways and I always confirm My wishes for you.

Chapter 8
Spiritual Power

Man is a spirit and has natural power. I add the spiritual power when needed. Those who call on Me will not be disappointed. Man-power is limited. Spiritual power is limitless. It can go far beyond your mind's comprehension.

Be open to receive all I have to offer. Fear of the unknown will hinder your chances of receiving.

I will mold you and prepare you for great works so that your faith can grow by leaps and bounds. What I need is your cooperation. Many of you have been showered with My gifts. It takes action on your part to put them into use. Pray before each endeavor and I will send out My angels to push back the evil spirits who try to thwart your works.

My righteous people have spiritual power. They only need to exercise it. Proof will be given to you for I make My truths known.

Your trust is the needed factor. Believe that whatever happens is for your own good and it will come to pass that way. Patience and endurance must continually be exercised.

Your latter years can be comforting when you have lived by following My laws. You will become full of wisdom and understanding. Even the demons will stop hanging around for they know that you recognize their existence and cast them out. Old age need not be dreaded when you live for Me.

Dreams of your future in the sky can raise your spirit. Great prizes are awaiting you for winning your races in life. Your memory will stay active when you acknowledge My presence at all times.

Do not hesitate to witness My goodness. You can be planting many seeds. People are becoming hungry in their spirit and your witnessing can feed their soul. I will add power to your spirit to make your words effective.

Dwell not on the past. It opens old wounds which I have healed. Be understanding and lend an ear to those who reminisce, but let the negative remarks fall by the wayside.

Keep love in your heart and it will replace all bitterness. Your spiritual mind will grow and grow when it feeds on love.

The mind and the soul must unite as one entity. I seek out those with spirituality and they become My candidates for power.

Be of good cheer with small gains. They all help in your quest of righteousness. I know what is in the heart. The world can be fooled but not your God.

Your eternal life is all that counts, so build up your faith through prayer,and spiritual power can be yours. The more you ask, the more you will receive. My children are not left orphans. I watch over them and send help when needed.

Let your spirit expand, with My Spirit giving you directions. Your trials may be many but your handling of them will show forth My glory.

Your goal of eternal life can be achieved if you keep your eyes on the cross. My people must be aware of My Son's sacrifice. Get the good news out by every possible means. I wish that all be saved and that none perish.

My Spirit can be had when you give your life entirely over to Me, holding nothing back. I will dwell in you in the person of the Holy Spirit and we can become one. My Spirit power will not be held from you and My gifts will be given out freely. You must believe to receive.

Be aware and alert of your capabilities. Take action to fulfill your new mission in life. We will work as a team to benefit mankind and show forth My glory.

Praise Me for I live within your praises. Lift up your hands with great exuberance and use the voice I have given you. It becomes sweet music to My ears.

You have been singled out individually and have My undivided attention in spite of the billions of people in the world.

I know your every thought and action but desire you to express them to Me. Our love affair will grow and grow with your intimate conversations. Listen often for My still small voice.

The people in the world are so busy but lovers take time out for one another. I look forward to the time that you spend with Me. No matter where you are, I am listening, for remember, I dwell within. A crowd of people should not hinder our talks.

Be mindful of the graces which I give out abundantly, not through your works, but by My choice.

Strive earnestly to live by My commandments. If My people would follow them, their lives could become more simple. Try to become perfect as I am perfect.

I am your rewarder. Since you have lived by My principles you wear the robe of righteousness and are entrusted with some of My riches. Enjoy them with continual praise on your lips, never forgetting your Father's love.

Pray for your less fortunate brethren. Ask for My mercy upon them, always keeping in mind that the soul is more important than the body.

Hardships bring a soul to Me. Unless one is drawn closer to Me, they walk in darkness. My light is needed to direct your every step. Walk with Me and you will want for nothing.

My wisdom is given to My faithful ones To be wise is a great asset in your world. Decisions can be made more readily and correctly. Insert little prayers throughout the day for My sanction upon your decisions.

Live each day as if it were your last. Your possessions would cease to be so important. Just let your spirit lead you, knowing My power is with you, for I am in you and you are in Me. This combination makes you a winner.

Do not allow the evil one to sway your thoughts. He will connive in every way possible to make you miserable. Praise Me in words and song and he will soon give up. It is when you listen that he sticks around. He would like to make you sick by planting wrong thoughts. Immediately erase the ideas he implants in your mind.

Rest your body and mind when you are tired. Know their limitations. I cannot work through someone who is worn out.

I need all My righteous to carry on My church. Get plenty of exercise to keep all the body parts functioning as they should. Walking each day is of prime importance, especially if you are talking with Me.

Listen attentively and you will learn My still small voice. A two way conversation is what I desire. Many of My faithful servants have discovered this intimate relationship.

With Your spirit and mine united, power becomes a part of

your spirit. Your words have power and My people detect this power because their spirit is in tune with the spiritual realm. To the unfaithful the words fall on deaf ears.

The spirit has unlimited growing power. The ears hear and the eyes see beyond the human limitations. Your faith has put into motion a purpose for your life and thus you are fulfilling My intent for your existence.

It is hard to fathom all the good that you can accomplish, but by following My ways and walking in them, step by step, My Father is pleased beyond measure.

Your life will never be free of troubles but I will make it satisfying. Your treasures in heaven are insurmountable. Never give up but keep pressing toward your high calling.

Goodness and kindness follow you because our spirits are united, I in you and you in Me. This thought alone can keep one on the straight and narrow path.

Your love for Me is only a shadow of the love I have for you. But your love can grow to a deeper depth with practice. Pray for a more perfect love and I will help in its perfection.

Remember all good things come from above. Give thanks throughout the day, naming your blessings. Taking them for granted stops the flow.

Your spiritual power can draw people to you. They will listen to what you have to say if they are hungering for righteous ness. I will open their ears if they have the right attitude.

Renew your Batismal vows. They are a guide to follow. Plus, read My word daily. I will speak to you through certain passages.

Develop good Christian friends and listen to what they say. You can continue to stay in the process of learning and be amazed at My confirmations which are spoken through them.

Ever learn to relax in My love. Erase all thoughts from your mind and fill them with "Jesus" thoughts.

Bask in your interpretation of what Heaven will offer. I will supply new insights to add to yours. Your moments of ecstasy will never cease.

Believe in My power working through you. Keep it activated through prayer. It can move mountains.

Chapter 9
Power Of The Tongue

The world was created through My words. My tongue spoke out the world's creation, thus signifying the great power in the tongue.

My children have inherited some of this power but at a far lesser scale. They can command evil spirits to leave in the name of "Jesus." Example: You spirits of (name the infirmity), I command you to leave in Jesus' name." In most cases the symptoms will lift. This method should be used at the first sign and with great authority. So many illnesses could be avoided if My children only knew the power of the tongue and exercised it.

It is spelled out in My word that greater works you will do for I go to My Father. You can also pray for others in My name and My anointing power will be given to perform miracles through My words spoken from your tongue.

Be not afraid of My power. Stand firm that your words can accomplish much. The requisite is a close relationship with Me.

True belief is a "must" to perform any ministry. Your love for Me is the driving force to win souls for My Kingdom.

Display the fruits of the spirit. People will recognize Me in you by your fruits. Remain humble as I exult you. Without My help you would fall.

The gift of the tongue is one of My many gifts. I speak through a mouth that is undefiled. My scriptures that are memorized and flow out of your lips become like music to My ears.

Using My words puts you in tune to the spiritual world. They are uplifting for your spirit. You can grow into My image as you repeat My words.

Meditating on the messages which My words convey keeps you in touch with the spiritual realm. Your faith can grow greatly with this practice.

Bask in the riches of My grace which I have poured out in abundance upon you. This gift will see you through all of your trials. As long as you are upon the earth you will not be free of them.

My attention is captivated through your prayers. I hear all your words spoken from your lips and know all your thoughts. Do not think that your prayers fall on deaf ears. My timing for your answers will come in due season.

Your ways for answered prayers may not be mine but I turn situations around in your best interest. Many years down the line you will understand.

Speak from the lips only positive affirmations. Too much negative can be brought into being. The evil one works on the words he hears coming from your tongue.

Think only positive thoughts and what you think will come out of your mouth. Your words can put into being things you thought impossible.

Speak health, no matter how you feel, and health can be in the making. Besides, people will enjoy being around you.

Those who curse and use My name in vain will be thrown in the lake of fire. Unless they make restitution and ask for forgiveness they are doomed.

Let your conversation be interesting to the listener, otherwise it is best to remain silent. Selfish people want to be heard all the time but a selfless person will do more listening.

Many times older people need a listening ear, so, for compassion, lend one. Offer it up as a prayer to Me and I will fill you with more patience.

Relax while living. I do not expect My faithful workers to overdo. Do not harbor guilt if you take time out from your ministry. Often one needs a diversion to receive new insight. I cannot fill a tired mind.

I am pleased when your tongue is used to praise Me. It should also be used in praise when speaking of others. Never spread rumors or speak ill of your neighbor. Have nothing to do with gossip.

If you follow My words, your words will have meaning. Your personality can be enriched and new friends shall be added. Your life can take on more meaning and excitement.

Pray about everything. Be not disappointed about any outcome. You have My assurance that I am in every situation. I can make good come from unwanted happenings. Your trust does much toward My working on your behalf.

Do not look for perfection in yourself. You will not enjoy the life that I expect should satisfy. Find humor in circumstance and laugh a lot. It can be medicine for both body and soul.

Keep an open mind and you will fill it with much diversion. Life can be made an interesting adventure. Your time on earth will fly fast and soon we shall meet face to face. I am looking forward to it and have a storehouse of wonderful things saved just for you. Your reunion day with Me will be far beyond your imagination. So keep fighting the good fight of faith.

Tell others of My mercy and goodness. Your witness of what I have done for you will help others to see the light. You can be planting seed for My Kingdom.

Branch out with other Christians. Let not "religions" hamper your work for Me. You can learn from one another.

Do not hesitate to speak out in My name. You may feel that you were talking to deaf ears but you have the power to open those ears. Some will think about what they heard at a later date and a conversion can begin.

Be a soul winner. I wish that none should perish. Each person has a free will and I will not stand in the way of how it is exercised. As people commit their lives to Me, I add them to My family. Their benefits become numerous.

When exercising your tongue be assertive and you will draw listeners. Weigh your words and keep them short. Even I get tired listening to long dissertations.

Your words express what is deep in your innermost being. They can be as sharp as any two-edged sword. Try to express My love and forgiveness to all people. Your words will be accomplishing My purpose and not come back to you void.

Keep walking with Me and your revelations will be numerous. I save My secrets for My faithful people to expound upon their content. They will only be given to those I trust to carry the messages. Whatever gifts they need to carry out My wishes will be added unto them.

Let contentment be your lot. Analyze not your situation but trust that I will bring the work which I have started in you to completion. Joy can penetrate your soul when you stop doing things your way.

What you say through your mouth is analyzed by your listeners. Let My love show forth through you. People are searching as never before. Your conversation should always stay on the positive side. Search your heart for new avenues to discuss. In prayerful meditation I will reveal them for you to explore and add wisdom. Anyone who comes to Me shall not be left empty.

Renew your Baptismal vows and recite them in true faith. Your words said from the heart bring great results.

Do not let your trust waver but hold fast to all My promises. Pray to the Holy Spirit to enlighten your mind before reading My word. Excitement will come to you as you see My word in different light. Read slowly and let My words dwell in you richly.

Choose your words before you speak. Let them come from the heart. Exercise this method and I will back those words with power. Your words can express My authority from on high. They will move the people whom I want moved.

Once you have given your life over to Me a brand new one will unfold before you. A warmth will fill your soul. You will know that I am with you. This comfortable feeling can be yours for the rest of your life.

Anyone who seeks Me will find Me. Their hearts and minds will become as one entity as they unite with Mine. This is My special gift reserved for My followers.

Without Me a person is nothing but with Me all things become possible. My truths, which I reveal to you, make you blessed, indeed.

As a man thinks in His heart, so his tongue tells on him. Be pure in heart and show to others that you and I are one.

My Father sent Me and I am sending you to gather souls to the Kingdom. The good news of eternal life must be spoken to others. Your words are seeds planted. Keep them flowing in love toward all people. Be not afraid for I am with you.

I will put words in your mouth that you were not thinking of saying. You will know by this that I am working in you and through you. Be not afraid of this gift. Consider yourself a chosen one.

Willing workers are needed for the time is getting short for My impending return. I do not wish that any shall perish. I love everyone, sinner as well as saint. But, I will not interfere with anyone's free will.

Pray for My people to turn from their wicked ways. You have no idea what your prayers can accomplish.

Let Me be your best friend. Listen for My still small voice so we can have a two way conversation. I have much to reveal to those who will pass on My word. They will become rich in grace. Their joy will ever increase. Those who want to be My anointed ones should ask and keep in prayer. Persistence draws you into My favor. Believe that you will receive and I will make it come to pass.

Chapter 10
Evangelistic Power

Evangelists are needed desperately in these latter days. My power will be poured out upon My faithful ones who spread My word. The ears of the lost will be open through it.

People sort out their priorities. The day at hand is now. Time is of the essence. Some are on their last chance. Delays may mean souls will be lost forever.

My gifted people should use their gifts and watch how I come through with power. They will be blessed one hundredfold when they keep their gifts in action.

It takes action on each one's part to do My work upon the earth. Live as I lived, loving everybody. Your example can be the best teacher for the observers. Let your light shine to become soul winners.

If you lean toward evangelization pray for enlightenment and guidance. Listen and I will speak to you in My still small voice. I will confirm your feelings through other Christians. Stay alert and live in the spiritual realm as well as the natural.

Support those you discern are true evangelists. You can do your part even though you do not possess the gift yourself. Your charity performed in My name will be credited to your account. No deed is left unnoticed by Me.

There are plateaus to be reach in heaven. Don't be satisfied in just making it into the gate but strive for a high place.

***

An evangelist can awaken the dormant state that keeps some people so complacent. They can stir up the fire within by getting it ignited within one's soul. They speak to the inner man. The hardened ones pay no heed in most cases but some souls are brought back to me. The words they hear convict them of their wrong doing. When they repent with a sincere heart I take them back with open arms. Those who commit their life to Me will feel My presence and their life will take on meaning.

***

My committed people are not left orphans. They are brought into My family and partake of all its blessings.

***

Learn all that you can about My life through the Holy Book and imitate Me. You will grow rich in My grace. Your life will become a journey back to Heaven.

***

My people receive a joy that is hard to express in worldly terms. The world's joy is fleeting but mine lasts even through one's trials.

***

My faithful pray when they are alone and thus loneliness is lifted. They are rewarded when they instigate prayer among others. Their prayers offered up for others bring great satisfaction to their soul.

***

When evangelists speak, My anointed ones are able to differentiate between truth and error. My gift of discernment will not be held back from those who seek it. Pray to ever expound in your faith.

***

A virtuous person can grow and grow but a sinful one stunts his growth. Stay ever in tune with My word and you will never have trouble sorting out good from evil.

***

People are known by the fruit they produce. Study the lives of the saints and you will discover that much good was accomplished by them. Some were very humble but I exalted them.

Be ever willing to be used as My instrument and your potential will be unlimited. Believe and you will receive. It is lack of faith that holds back all I have to offer. I am a generous God and desire to show My generosity to all.

My faithful ones can become evangelizers. I will add My power along with any effort one makes to spread My word. The good news must be spread far and wide. Hearers can benefit if they want to listen.

Each is given a little faith and each must work at developing it. My faithful ones can be instrumental in increasing faith in others through diligent effort.

Pray for My words. My Spirit dwelling in you will prompt you, adding wisdom to your other spiritual gifts.

Growth can be an ongoing adventure. You are in control of the speed. The more time that you spend in My spiritual realm, praying for My people, the more you will grow in My image .

Love is the key which unlocks many doors and eventually will unlock the gate to heaven. Whatever you do for any of My people, you do for me.

Being busy does not hold any of My righteous back because every moment can be a prayer if offered up to Me. Your mundane tasks can be accomplished with ease, knowing that I see all and understand what you are going through. Your heart is My gauge of your love.

Be not troubled but hold fast to your faith. Run the race with great endurance. Faint not, but keep going for My name's sake. Some day it will be worth it all.

The evil one tries to keep you idle but do not give in to laziness. Rest is essential, but continual rest you do not need. Likewise, wasting time on worldly things keeps your mind off Me. Be cognizant of Me at all times and I will be in the center of your life.

My ways become your ways as My Spirit directs your spirit. Your followers will be many because spirits unite.

Spread the word as you travel down My path of life. It is the only sure way to eternity. Take as many people with you by not being afraid to speak out in My favor. Holding back may send some to their doom.

Be moderate in speech. A little said can plant a seed which I will water. Let love dominate your speech. Others will not be offended. Pray for the qualities needed to win souls. I will not hold back the essentials when your heart is right.

You must be humble. Anything put on for show is frowned upon by Me and I will not be in it. Stay close in prayer at all times and you will know My will. Your own soul will be satisfied. Dissatisfied people are not walking in My will.

Be content no matter what position you play in life. Experience often is needed for your training toward My greater gifts. Accept what happens with patience and endurance. Joy can flood your soul in spite of hardships.

Bear one another's burdens and do not find fault in My people. Elaborate only on their good points. Leave any judging up to Me. Only I know what is truly in a person's heart. Further, not all circumstances leading to a person's actions may be known. So be still rather than speak out wrongly.

Silence is golden at times. Be a good listener, as it helps people pour out their troubles. As you practice My principles, your reward will be great in heaven.

Anything My people can do to spread the good news will be personally blessed by Me. A ministry can be formed by your own efforts. Your service is needed. Unselfishness leads to new life in Me. Experiencing this life brings a happiness that the world cannot give.

My presence becomes more real as your faith grows. Our friendship supplies your daily needs.

One cannot trust human love, but divine love is yours for the asking. Remain sinless to receive this love to the fullest.

Praise Me for your newfound love which will grow deeper and deeper as the years go by. Old age need not hinder you from spreading My love. Your life can be a good example of what My love can do for those who commit themselves entirely to Me.

As one relaxes in My love, trials are taken in stride. By offering up the bad times to Me, they become prayers. Our hearts unite as one. Inwardly you know that all is well and eternal life is your goal that you sought after and won. There is no doubt in your heart. Your older years can be happy with great hope in your heart. With this anticipation you can win others to My Kingdom.

A positive attitude produces a happy heart. Never let doubt and negative thoughts surface. Fight them as a plague. The evil one tries to pull you down to his level. Do not fall for his tactics.

Let your voice ring with good cheer for you carry My good news. Your happiness can become infectious. Love can dominate your life and those around you.

Temper disappears when My heart and yours unite as one. A new life is obtainable in your world. My Son made this possible by His horrible suffering and death.

Anyone who asks forgiveness can experience a new life or rebirth. Those who reject My Son reject Me and they will be doomed for all eternity.

My faithful ones have a responsibility to inform the unsaved. Ask for the means to help spread My word and I will not hold back.

Anyone who seeks to win souls is an evangelizer. When their heart is right, I add power to their words. My people know when My words flow through them. Workers are needed in these end times for I wish that none shall perish.

When one devotes his or her life to Me, I can use that person in extraordinary ways. There are testing periods which one must survive to withstand My work. Those who do will receive more power from on high.

Transgressions will be forgotten when hearts have turned to Me. Goodness and mercy will follow them. The old ways will cease for behold I have made all things new.

Give praise and thanks for the change in your life. I live among the praises of My people. Blessed are they who walk in My Godly counsel. All training is a stepping stone for gifts to come. Your willingness will indeed be rewarded.

I continue to lift people on higher planes, drawing them ever so close to Me. You radiate light to shine in your darkened world. Do not hibernate but let your light brighten others' paths so they will not lose their way.

Live one day at a time with peace in your heart. Peace can flow out like a river when your heart is right. You can spread happiness by your attitude. Work diligently on loving people and friendships will grow.

Loneliness is lifted when the mind is taken off self. The effort to love My people becomes a force in your control. This is due to My power working through you.

Fix your spiritual eyes on Me each day. Make Me the center of all your actions. They will receive My personal direction.

Be not melancholy, for this is giving in to the evil one. He is in the world and wants you to be miserable. Prayer lifts your mind out of this state.

Let your body be a living sacrifice by using it for the good of others. You will be blessed beyond measure when you put others' needs before your own. You become My pearl of great price.

Come, let us reason together. Practicing My presence brings assurance that all is well. I have come to make peace. If turmoil is present, evil is working against you. Use the power I have given you to cast the darkness out and My words and light will filter in.

Pray continually for more power. Acknowledge the Holy Spirit within you and talk to Him as a person. Even though the Trinity is united as one, We are three Divine Persons and like to be addressed as such. Mention Our names often as you pray. A conversation becomes more personal when a name is used.

People in your world like their names to be used. Try to remember names. Seal each one in a prayer for better remembrance. Take your mind off self when introduced and repeat the name silently several times. It takes practice but your memory will improve.

My power can do wonders to the memory. Just keep asking and more will be given to you .

Thank the Holy Spirit for His teaching and reproof. He is helping to mold you into My image. Since I and My Father are one, you can become one with Us.

Thank My Father for the beauty in your world. He created it all and His intent was for peoples' enjoyment. Speak to Him about His creations. He has a listening ear. He sleeps not and goes to and fro throughout the earth observing each one individually. He has this ability because of His great power.

Be a believer and your faith will grow rapidly along with My wisdom. A wise man is rich in My blessings. He does not waste his time on the foolish things of this world. He spends time loving My people in a variety of ways, applying the fruits of the spirit. His friends become many along life's journey. My power will be upon him because he remains righteous.

I will continually work on your heart if you keep committing yourself to Me. The mind and heart must be willing and open for the tasks set before them and operate according to My word. Love must always be present.

Only I know what is taking place in each one's heart. So, never judge your neighbor. Be kind to your enemies and I will work on their hearts. Only pay back evil with good.

Renew your baptismal vows and you will be washed in the water of life and cleansed from unrighteousness. I want you to work toward your perfection. You can start on your glorification while on earth.

Stay holy and My goodness and mercy will follow you all the days of your life. Your heavenly abode is being prepared. You cannot fathom what awaits you. Your eternal ecstasy will far exceed anything that you have experienced on earth.

A little daydreaming about eternity will help you get through your rough moments on earth. When people remain true to Me, their life in eternity will be complete bliss. My power carries you through impossible situations. The grace it imparts strengthens you to accomplish My purpose.

Experiencing My power is exciting. The wonders you can perform under My anointing is incomprehensible. Pray to receive all I have to offer. Believe, and watch how things unfold in your favor.

My righteous are gainers. Their faith keeps them on My narrow path. Their goal is to obtain their eternal life with Me.

Satisfaction is obtained in this world and complete happiness in the next.

My children must believe My promises in My word. Sin separates us but righteousness unites us.

Develop a personal relationship with Me and you will not be lonely. Talk with Me like you talk with your best friend. Everything you say is held in My heart. I can relieve your anxieties. Talking over problems with Me has My listening ear.

The gifts of the Spirit are many. Speak of Me often to others. You will know by the words coming from your mouth whether you have the gift of evangelism. Thank Me for every gift that you recognize and use the gifts wisely.

Pray for the gift of discernment so that you can separate truth from error. Remember the devil goes about in your world as a deceiver, often disguising himself as an angel of light.

Take time to read My word. You will not perish for lack of knowledge. Follow My ways read in the Gospels. You do not pay back those who have done evil to you. Do good to your enemies and pray for them. Then good will overcome evil.

My people who spread the gospel must be well versed in My word. They must be able to differentiate between My promptings and that of the evil one. Many of My people listen to Bible tapes. This is a good practice and the mind and soul can absorb truth and not fight against one another.

Time should be used wisely. The evil one enters when the mind is left to roam. My word, prayer, and good literature feeds the soul and mind.

Talking to Me releases tension but talking with a neighbor

can become tiring because words are usually weighed in the mind.

I repeat nothing and hold what you say in My heart. Your problems can be left with Me and the mind set free.

If decisions need to be made, pray about them first. I will then be in whatever you decide. Putting off often causes much confusion. You may think that you decided wrongly but eventually you will see that My favor was upon it.

Always stay close to Me, remaining free from sin. If you should slip, ask My forgiveness immediately. Separation from Me becomes a great loss to you.

I bless My people who spread My word and remain My companion. They are accumulating great riches in their future life with Me. You will find out the truth I am conveying when I call you home.

The time on earth is fleeting so make the most of it. Your benefits will far outweigh the inconveniences that you are experiencing in your present life.

Chapter 11
Teaching Power

The person who reads My words, listens to them, and abides by them, becomes equipped to teach. One who steps out in My name to proclaim the gospel will be given special power to convey My messages. My anointing will be upon him or her. Initiate the action and I will follow through with My gifts.

Patience is a virtue that must be exercised. Remember your listeners are from diverse backgrounds and cannot grasp all that you say in one hearing. It takes much repetition on your part.

My teachers can plant the seeds and I will do the cultivating. I can open the ears of those I choose and give them a mind to understand spiritual knowledge.

There will be scoffers, but pay them no heed. Evil lurks in those who refuse to turn from sin.

Those who listen to get their hearts satisfied will not go away hungry. It is more important to feed the soul than the body. Your soul lives on forever and ever.

Keep yourself in My word and I will give you the energy to release your knowledge. Excuses are not accepted by Me. To those who apply effort to their gift, more will be given them. For those who do not use their gifts lose what they have been given.

I am a generous God and will honor My faithful people. I desire to give gifts but many do not accept them. It grieves Me when people become so indifferent in spiritual matters.

Spend time gaining My knowledge and pass it on generously. You will be the gainer in the long run and receive blessings from those you train. Their expression of inquisitiveness will make you want to satisfy their hunger.

Anything you do for My people is honored by My Father in heaven. His love for you will grow even greater as you utilize your time in spreading the word. You will know the impact which you had on people on your judgment day.

Those who go the extra mile are blessed exceedingly. My love will shine forth in their face. Reach out continually in faith and My presence will follow you.

The righteous have My protection and doubly so when they have a personal relationship with Me. Our running conversations will keep you in My spiritual flow.

My Heavenly Father's love is far greater then any earthly love. Our preparation for your heavenly abode is continually taking place. You will want for nothing. Your hopes and dreams will be more than satisfied.

But on earth I cannot promise you a bed of roses. The evil one prowls around to see whom he can make miserable. I will comfort you through his attacks and give you strength to bear all your burdens.

Happy is the person who fears Me. He will delight in My ways and make them his ways. He will understand that I make all things turn out for his own good.

So, be of good courage and enjoy one day at a time. Keep a positive attitude and others will enjoy being around you.

Happy are they who know My will and follow in My footsteps. They will aspire in their present life and be working toward their glorification. My number system has perfect calculations.

When people listen to My anointed ones, they are moved to repent. Their ears will be open if they take action. They can drink from My well that will never run dry.

My words can satisfy their hungry hearts. They will not be robbed of their salvation once they turn to Me.

My teachers are equipped by Me to win souls through My power given them. They absorb My word and pass it on. The world should not stand in their way or they will lose My power. For those who use what has been given them, more will be added. Out of their mouths will flow My words. They will not come back void but accomplish My purpose.

I am aware of My workers' intentions. They must pray to have all pure motives. Satan tries to catch them off guard. It is so important to stay in My grace at all times. Sin will pull one into the evil one's gravity. Without My grace, darkness will envelop you. A person can become trapped in the snares of evil. The lies spoken in one's mind are confusing.

My words spoken from your lips will lift darkness. Hearing My anointed teachers will help your understanding. Do all in your power to increase your spirituality.

My people press toward their high calling in spite of adversities. Their love for Me spurs them on. We become one in spirit. Our love grows deeper as the years go by. Be not dismayed by any happenings. They are ordered by the Lord to strengthen you and keep you on the straight and narrow path.

Let your mind develop with your spirit and become united. Righteousness will be your lot. Evil cannot win over goodness. Satan will try working on the mind but he cannot conquer the mind when it has been grounded in the spirit. He will not cease to try, so be not troubled when he enters your thoughts but cast him out, ignoring all his ideas.

My anointed teachers can help your friends so invite them to listen to those who help you walk the path of faith. Their ears, too, will open in time. At least, you will be planting seed. The growth will come to those who are open to truth.

I will make your conversations exciting when you hold the Trinity in your talks. All three of us are available to heap grace upon you .

Man is a spirit and only things of the spirit will satisfy the soul. The flesh can only be satisfied for short periods and thirst will come again. I am the living water that satisfies. Those who drink from My well will receive the water of life. They will live forever.

Your heart and My heart will beat as one. Our love can continue to grow. Moments of ecstasy can be yours even in your world. This is possible when you ask in expectancy. Close your eyes, take deep breaths and rest in Me.

If My young people would learn more of Me and follow in My ways, they would not be so apt to gratify the flesh. Their spirit needs to grow. They will discover that I am the way, the truth, and the life. No one can return to My Father except through Me. I have been given the power to judge the living and the dead.

Seek Me, My children, and much will be added to your lives. I stand at your door and knock, waiting for you to let Me in. I will not intrude where I am not wanted.

When you show your availability, I will teach you through the Holy Spirit whom I send to dwell within you. He will be your guide and comforter. Shun not His presence for I will give you the eyes and ears of understanding. Your spiritual gifts will see you through all your adversities.

The evil one cannot penetrate the souls of My righteous. They may be tried and tempted but they come through in their shining armor which they have learned to put on each day.

Life is a spiritual battle. Putting on the armor of faith wards off the darts of the devil. You can become victorious by building up your faith, from mustard seed size to giant proportions.

Pray continually for more faith. It can take you through all your problems. Believe and you will receive. The doubters lose out on My grace.

Live in expectancy of My gifts. I will not let you down. I am with My righteous in everything they do. They need not feel alone. Reach out to others with the love I have afforded you. To those who are given much, much is expected.

I am your healer. If you trust Me, I will favor you with healings. Some diseases I take away from My people before they are aware of them. So continue thanking Me for known and unknown healings.

Do not let yourself get so busy that you have no time to converse with Me. I anxiously await our conversations. I listen to everything you have to say and remember every detail. Nothing escapes My ears.

Listen to My teachings. You can learn much. I came onto the earth to save My people. I also taught them how to live. If they follow My way they can cope with any situation. Life need not be as hard as My people make it.

So often "self" takes first place. Unhappiness develops because "self" can never be satisfied. Let Me occupy first place and happiness will abound. I can fill the lowly with My ways and they can rise above all their problems. Reaching out to others takes the mind off "self". I can heal the broken-hearted but they must stay close to Me. Let Me set you free in your everyday life.

The anxieties for a more stable life can be erased. Through My teachings one learns to relax and live one day at a time. Placing your cares in My hands and trusting Me give you a freedom that you never dreamed you could possess.

Love My people and you will love yourself. Ask for My power to sustain you and you will receive more than enough. Your breathing will become normal and your health will flourish.

The power given My children helps them to live their life victoriously. Out of their innermost being flows My living water. They are constantly being cleansed. The sins of the flesh will gradually disappear by my children's own will.

My people can become saints through the power of My grace. Abide in Me and I'll abide in you and we will entwine as one.

Hearts are transformed by My power. Family and friends will notice this transformation. You become a powerful witness for My honor and glory. Your life will not be lived in vain.

Happy are they who believe what My words convey. The promptings of Satan cannot alter their minds. Since they pay him no heed, they are not dragged down to his level. He will soon flee to someone else who will believe his lies.

Keep always in the positive realm and your spirit will be united with mine. Your happiness will prevail.

Trust Me completely and worry will no longer hold you captive. Commit every bit of your life to Me and watch how I work in your favor. You may not agree in My ways but believe Me, it is all for your good. Your soul is much more important than your body. I desire your salvation above everything else. My love will always be with you. I will never leave you or forsake you.

It is only when My people sin and want no part of Me that I leave them alone. But when they call on Me and ask forgiveness from their heart, I take them back into My fold.

I expect the love I afford you to be passed on to others. You will remain in the happy realm when you abide by My expectations. Your actions become a powerful witness for Me as I send power through you. Some words that you use have been ordered by Me. So do not be surprised when My words flow out of your mouth.

My people need to know about My deep love for them. Hesitate not to inform them. You may be their only source.

Continue with your growth in faith. You will find the time for earthly things will grow dim in your sight. Your comprehension of the spiritual realm will become more keen as My power continues to flow through you.

The evil one will try to distract you in every possible form but you must ignore him. His lies are constantly deceiving.

Your already acquired knowledge should keep you joyful. Rejoice that I have favored you with insight. Praise Me throughout the day and I will stay at your side listening. Evil will depart from your presence. The devil's demons must bow to the name of Jesus. They become weary of doing so and depart.

You can control the forces around you. My power makes this possible. Continue to pray for My power. I will not withhold anything good that you ask of Me.

My people are rich in My sight but lose some of their riches when doubt enters their minds and they entertain it.

A positive attitude will take you above all negative thinking if you have the will to change. Let Me be your anchor. You will not drift to and fro. I can keep you stable in all of your ways.

Confide in Me and answers will come in diversified ways. Your life can become exciting watching for them.

Remain teachable, with an open mind. I can fill it with knowledge. You will become wise in the process. Those who listen to My words are not left empty. Their growth becomes an ongoing adventure.

Those who seek Me will find Me. I am always available but will only enter your abode on invitation. I dwell within My righteous. Their protection becomes unlimited.

I see all and know all. Nothing can be hidden from Me. The fear of Me is the beginning of wisdom. Accepting My teaching is faith personified.

For those who build up their faith willingly, I am delighted indeed. I will furnish the tools they need to keep going. They will not lack for information.

Let not your heart be troubled with things of the world. Behold, all will become new. Contentment can be yours if you faint not. Ever walk on the lighted path I have set before you.

Renewing your mind daily in My word is your hope of glory. Joy can permeate your entire being when you put Me first in your life. A committed life to Me receives My fervor.

Learn to listen when you are out with friends. By thinking what you want to say during their conversations often causes you to miss what I want to tell you through them

Some hurting people just need a good listening ear. It helps relieve their anxieties. In the process you will be using your love gift and I will add more. To whom much is given, much is required. Happiness becomes a way of life when operating in My gifts.

While expanding in the spiritual gifts, beware of attacks from the enemy. Prayer strengthens you to withstand all his conniving. I, the Holy Spirit, lead you to your salvation.

The times are evil but you must learn to relax to stay well. Worrying will do you no good. It is only when you trust Me that worry is lifted.

A real understanding of your purpose on earth will lead you away from earthly things. I lift you up on a higher plane where peace and joy are obtainable. Work diligently on spreading My word and you will lack for nothing. Listen to the Holy Spirit for constant guidance. He will teach you if you acknowledge Him and practice listening as you would to a companion. He will become your best friend.

With the Holy Spirit's teachings, you become wise. His gifts are wisdom, piety, knowledge, counsel, fortitude, understanding, and fear of the Lord. Possessing these gifts will make you one with the Father, Son, and Holy Spirit.

My people find My teachings hard to believe, but, once I reveal Myself to them, what a difference it makes in their faith. Great is one's faith who believes with no revelations.

Always ask the Holy Spirit for strength when you have overwhelming tasks that must be accomplished. You will be amazed at the power that you can possess. Never fail to thank Him for His favor in granting your requested power. Without this power you could become sick from exhaustion.

Chapter 12
Heart Power

A loving heart energizes the soul. There is My power in love, producing tenderness and compassion. When you touch My hurting people, you can soothe their aching hearts as I let My power flow through you.

A hardened heart must become softened. A number of people mellow with age but others will not listen. They will become doomed in the lake of fire. Their free will leads them to destruction.

Those who have My gift of love must spread it around for it can become contagious. People should undo the shackles that hold them bound to this world. Satan is always pushing you from Me. Prayer can loose his hold.

When your heart is conformed to Mine, it generates power. Your love is lifted out of the natural and transformed gradually into one with supernatural qualities. My will becomes your will and we become as one.

Your footsteps are blessed wherever you walk so do not hesitate to spread My word. Through your love, My love will be shown.

Diversify your time and spend some alone with Me. I am a jealous God and desire your attention and love. During our intimate conversations you will be receiving a healing for your ills. Just relaxing in My love has healing properties for the body and soul.

Also, spend some time releasing love to others. You will find that you will get back more than you give. I have My own ways for rewarding My faithful ones.

Learning how to live My way early in life makes your latter years meaningful. You will know that you have not lived in vain and you will be at peace with your conscience.

Do not waste time with friends that bleed your energy. You can shorten your conversations when you realize that they are not listening. But do lend an ear to their needs and give a little advice through your own wisdom. A shooting prayer for the right words on your lips helps tremendously.

Never shun your duties in spreading My word. If you are being paid for work, do not take that paid time to speak of Me. I will not bless those words. Example will convey My message.

When you are walking down My path of life for you, you will experience much peace. Where peace is present there is My presence also. Take deep breaths knowing your body is functioning in a normal fashion.

Worldly people are in constant battle. It takes a toll on the body in time. The evil one will stick around when he sees destruction in the process.

Stop and take inventory of your life often. If love is the common denominator, you are on the right track. My power is added to your love, causing it to grow. The good that your love portrays is immeasurable.

Keep in mind to rest often in My love to prevent body burnout. You will automatically slow down when thoughts of Me are present.

The world is in much turmoil. Going along the worldly way will keep you in this state. When you learn how to switch to the spiritual realm in prayer you have made great strides in earthly living.

—◦◦◦—

Think positive and the results will astound you. As a person thinks, so is he. Happiness prevails in a positive thinker. His friends become many.

—◦◦◦—

Set goals in life and you will be amazed at the power I give to achieve them. I wish for My children to have the desires of their heart. If their heart is right I intervene to satisfy it. A thankful heart will keep receiving.

—◦◦◦—

Those who know how to love can endure all things. My help and power is ever available. Never be hesitant to ask. My listening ear is in reach of all My righteous.

—◦◦◦—

Your heart and mine can beat as one. This releases great power. My people do not seem to realize the vast amount of gifts available to them.

—◦◦◦—

Reading My word daily will give you new insights in the spiritual realm. If you are seeking for answers you will find them in the scriptures. Also, listen for My still small voice. I wish to reveal secrets to you.

—◦◦◦—

Experiencing My presence is a great accomplishment. It alone, when recognized, can give you real ecstasy. Our companionship can grow as the years roll by and your joy will ever increase. Life need not be dull when you have Me at your side.

—◦◦◦—

There are great wonders yet to be explored and you can be in on much excitement. Only believe and watch how I make My words come to pass. My words never come back to Me void but will always accomplish their purpose.

—◦◦◦—

Always be ready for your homecoming. No one knows the hour but happy are they who are prepared. There is much celebration as each soul enters heaven. Your mansion is in the preparation stage. My storehouse is full of gifts to shower upon you. Think on these words when you are burdened with life's problems. Time is fleeting. Your salvation and that of others should be your only vital concern.

I will help you with any spiritual need. Just make your request known to Me. I know your wants but want to hear them uttered from your lips. You must initiate an action and I will follow through. If your request would be detrimental to the soul, it will not be granted.

All My people can be used for the vital work of spreading the gospel, no matter the position in life. Words and example are two important tools. Words are seeds planted and they need not be many. Just pray for My cultivation. I will not disappoint you. I delight in watching your faith grow.

When your heart is right there is power to heal the body. My righteous people have much going for them. Their bodies function in a normal fashion. There is nothing worse than anger to throw off the chemistry of the body. Fear also has a deadly effect.

You do your body a favor when you control your temper and keep calm in the midst of storms. This can be accomplished with My help and power which I give out freely to those who believe and trust.

Your faith must continue to grow. Then living will become an adventure, not a drudgery. Spread yourself out to acquire new friends and let your Christian light shine forth. You will be planting seed in My vineyard.

When your heart is right, your body cooperates. Health can be yours. Speak it out with positive affirmations. Negative words should not be in your vocabulary.

Positive words generate their own power and added to mine bring overwhelming results. Happy are they who walk blamelessly toward their goal. Their eternal life is already sealed in this world.

Give generously while you can and your bank account will never run dry. I have My own means for multiplying. You are rich, indeed, to know and understand My methods.

When your heart and mine beat as one you will have heart power. What you desire in your heart can come to pass. Prayer and sacrifice are tools added for your use.

With love power, your love for all people goes beyond human capabilities and so does your compassion. Your love grows into Christlike love. A greater love had no man than My Son. He suffered and died to save all people.

Never fail to thank Him for bringing you into this realization. Your mind can grow and grow to comprehend the spiritual values I release to you.

Overcoming the world is a great achievement brought about by your will and My power. Joy is yours to cherish. Let not the evil one rob you with his lies. Fight with My words in casting him out.

Your plateaus of achievements will reach higher levels. Ever keep climbing. Your holiness is a great asset toward your sanctification.

When we see face to face, your journey will be complete. Then ecstasy will be yours forever and ever.

Be of exceedingly great courage. No one can take My gifts from you. Use them wisely. They add to your joy. Be ever thankful that I have found favor in you.

Tell of My gifts so others will seek them. Their desire for Me will be mine and I will fill it. No one who comes to Me will walk away empty. My grace is given out abundantly.

The heights in heaven are far beyond your comprehension. Reach for a high place, and if you go beyond your call of duty, I will honor your sacrifices. My people are never left unrewarded.

Let your generous heart govern your actions. It will receive power from on high to accomplish what you thought to be impossible. These accomplishments will keep you going from glory to glory.

You can float above your problems with great ease because you know I hold your future in the palm of My hand. Everything will work for good for you even though you do not understand your present circumstance. When we see face to face you will comprehend in an instant why trials had to befall you.

I should increase as you decrease. You can go from selfishness to selflessness and joy will stay with you. The change may be gradual but you will benefit exceedingly from it.

Always remember that life is short compared to eternity. There is everlasting ecstasy in heaven. By living a sinless life on earth, your glorification is in the process. You can obtain a direct route to heaven with no stopover.

No more tears will be shed when you reach My destination. Only complete happiness will prevail forever and ever. So do not let your problems overwhelm you. They are leading you to your crown. Rejoice in the middle of tribulation. It will lessen the blows in your life.

Praise Me often with a song in your heart. Negative thoughts can be erased in this manner. You can create your own joy through righteous living and it cannot be taken from you.

Gifts which I give remain with you unless you abuse them. They were given for a purpose and should be used rightly. I will show you how to use them and prompt you along the way. When you walk in My light you receive some sight in the spiritual world. Your understanding is also made more keen.

My people have much to gain. Unfortunately, they are not aware of all I have to offer. Some even feel unworthy to ask. Let Me be the judge. Just ask and see for yourself how I unfold your needs. It may not be immediate but I have a due season.

Remembering that My presence is within you should bring much satisfaction to your soul. Many of your counterparts have not the joy that you possess. They seek it in worldly pleasures but do not find it and often, in so doing, bring damnation to their soul.

It is your duty to pray diligently for the conversion of sinners. I acknowledge My righteous people's prayers. In so doing you bring much peace to your own soul. Your time is not wasted. Blessed are all your efforts to save souls.

Let a loving heart rule you and it will receive power from on high. This power is felt by My faithful people and they rejoice with grateful hearts. They are not afraid to step out in faith and perform in My name. I will allow miracles to happen as proof of My glory and reward for your faithfulness.

Chapter 13

Faith Power

The reward for building your faith is My power. Anyone who seeks will find. The effort put forth to increase faith receives My sanction. I will perform special acts through My people of great faith. They will know and recognize My power working through them, for I use them as My vessel. Their own power could not accomplish My purpose.

Never fail to thank Me for My gifts, for they are not limited to just one. The more gifts that you are given, the more power you receive. So, great works can be performed by you.

Remain humble when power is sent through you and realize that by yourself you can do nothing. It is our oneness that brings about marvelous wonders.

Stay ever so close to Me to keep the power working. Your friends and acquaintances will greatly benefit from your gifts. The more you are in the Spirit, the more I will increase your wattage of power.

Let not the worldly things keep you away from My work. There is so much to be done and so little time left.

Help My people see the light by your faith. They do not have to walk in darkness. Speak up for My sake and your words will become anointed. Power accompanies My anointing and many blessings will come your way.

The doubts which the evil one is planting at this very moment will draw you further away from Me if you succumb to them. Life is a constant battle but you can end up a victor if you faint not. Build up your faith constantly and your courage will accompany it.

I do not promise an easy life for My righteous, but I do promise one of fulfillment if you walk in My ways. Feelings of accomplishment far outweigh pleasures. The joy I relinquish is all you need.

I am creating new hearts from seeds which you are planting. Do not grow weary of your well-doing. You may feel criticized at times but recognize where it is coming from. Press on toward your high calling.

Keep your spiritual ears open for My still small voice. I will tell you when to stand still and when to go forward. Patience can be practiced in the interim.

My power will not be withheld from My faithful people. Believe this statement and you will find out the electrifying effect it has upon your body and spirit. Your strength will surprise even you. I wish to be your helper so, for this reason, I sent you the Holy Spirit to supply all your needs. Never fail to give thanks to Him.

Always recognize the Trinity's presence, Father, Son, and Holy Spirit. Lonesomeness will vanish when you know all three of Us desire your company. As this fact sinks into your spirit, you will want more and more to separate yourself from the world and spend time with Us. Your spirit will rise to new heights bringing many moments of contentment.

Your world will not understand these deep feelings you have toward Us. Your latter years will benefit greatly from our relationship. There will be no conscience to prick you when you remain righteous. Sinners can become saints walking the earth. Your example can lead many to My Kingdom.

If you slip down from the world's pressures, a contrite heart will bring My forgiveness. Only I know what is truly in a person's heart. There are many in the world who go through religious rituals, but are not made right with Me. Woe to them on the day of judgment. They are only interested in man's concept of them.

Call on the Trinity and power will surge throughout your whole being. My believers with great faith get results. Any tinge of unbelief nullifies My gifts.

My grace is sufficient to get you through any hardship. With grace you are endowed with power. By yourself you can do nothing but, with My power, all things are possible.

Remain sinless and stay close to Me and watch how I work through you. It is exciting to be placed in My honorable positions. Always be submissive to My will.

Test the spirits if you are not sure of your next move. I will reveal Myself or give confirmations through others.

Stay in prayer as much as you are able. The evil one cannot stand to hear you pray and you prevent him from penetrating your mind with his lies. The scriptures that you quote act as your sword in battle. Every one recited is a thrust toward the enemy pushing him further away. Your faith is your armor and the darts he throws bounces off your coat of protection. No one can afford to be without this protection.

Those who fail to call on Me are left groping in the dark. Without My power they will keep walking in the dark and eventually slip and fall. I light My righteous people's paths. They see and do not stumble. How blessed are the feet that trod on My paths.

Tribulations will come but you have nothing to fear. You have been set free. Praise and thank Me and with your freedom pass the good news of the gospel to others. You can do much for the unsaved. A kind word or smile are starters to gain confidence. Always stay in the patient zone to build up your endurance.

~~~

My storehouse is overflowing with blessings in both your present life and your future with Me. You are fortunate, indeed.

~~~

Count your blessings and be not envious of your neighbor. You have no idea what that person is going through. People are good actors and put on a front for show. They often joke around but are crying on the inside. So do not judge, but pray for everyone. The prayers of the righteous do much good.

~~~

When your life is unfolded before you on Judgment Day you will be glad that you interceded for so many people. Many will thank you personally and will be so grateful both in their present life and the eternal one. Because of your faith you have the power to accomplish much while on the earth. Exercise it and see for yourself how I work through you.

~~~

If things do not work out the way you prayed, just remember that My ways are not your ways. Only I know what is best for a person's well-being.

~~~

Be sensitive to the Holy Spirit as He teaches you in the way you are to go. He will admonish you when needed. One often gets His still small voice mixed up with the conscience. His voice will usually come to you through sentences.

~~~

Test the Spirit by asking questions. He will identify Himself but the evil spirit will not answer. Use the name of Jesus often. The evil one flees at the sound of the name of Jesus.

~~~

Treasure your faith power for it is indeed a gift. Many people cannot understand what you do. They possess not the spiritual eyes and ears of understanding. To them you speak foolishness. Pay them no heed, as you are rich beyond measure.

~~~

Be holy as I am holy. My power given you from on high

will help you accomplish this purpose. You can be trusted with My revelations.

—⟡—

Truth will conquer error. Much is being written but unfortunately not all is true. Interpretation of My word is being garbled.

—⟡—

My holy people receive with their spiritual eyes and ears true meaning. Keep attuned to My world. The world's allurements will grow dim in your sight.

—⟡—

Reach out to My hurting people in numerous ways. I will give you the boldness, and place the words in your mouth. Bring souls to Me and your stay on earth will not be in vain. Your happiness will increase and your own life will be made more interesting. Push on toward your high calling. When your race in life is finished, your awards will be many.

—⟡—

Master the art of prayer. Your relatives, friends, acquaintances, and even strangers can become benefactors.

—⟡—

Prayer can be said among crowds as well as in your own quiet spot. I hear all your words and delight in your faith. My favor rests upon all My faithful. Their security is eternal life.

—⟡—

Keep yourself motivated and set goals for your life. The Holy Spirit whom I sent to dwell within you will help you meet your goals, providing your motives are pure and holy. You will be amazed how much you can accomplish with spiritual help.

—⟡—

Be humble through every achievement for, without My spiritual help, you would eventually fall. You are walking in My light and see and hear with the eyes and ears I have given you. Consider yourself rich beyond measure.

—⟡—

You may wonder why people can't understand some things you say but they have not as yet been blessed with the spiritual senses. Continue praying for them and keep planting seed.

Never give up on anyone. They may be just a prayer away.

Oftentimes your words will fall by the wayside, but your prayers will not. The prayers of a righteous man availeth much. There is prayer depth to obtain and the more one prays, the greater the chances for obtaining that depth.

My peace has different levels and you can receive greater peace according to the time spent in prayer. My word tells you to pray without ceasing. So sort out your priorities and move toward that holy life which I am drawing you to fulfill. Your happiness will increase one hundredfold.

The power which you generate from holiness will be lasting power. It will not be taken from you. Your prayers for others will always contain power. My prayer warriors can move mountains. Obstacles of great magnitude are removed. The good that they do runs far beyond their imagination.

One can experience glory on earth through My revelations. These come in numerous ways: through My word, visions, dreams, My still small voice, and confirmations from others. You can live from glory to glory with anticipated excitement.

To get to this point, it takes concentrated effort on your part by sorting out priorities. Time spent in the spiritual realm will bring great satisfaction. Outside of prayer, helping others will put you in that realm when you offer the work up to Me. You can actually feel My presence through your performance. I give you added strength in the process.

Praise Me for My workings through you. Remember, I and My Father are one and we often manifest ourselves through the Holy Spirit. He, too, is one with Us.

Let your faith power grow by continually building up your spirit. No one can rob you of your faith when it is grounded in my word. There is no limit on your growth in the spiritual realm.

Chapter 14
Visionary Power

When My righteous people show great devotion through prayer and meditation, and practice My presence for long durations, I choose a certain few to see through their spiritual eyes. I lift the darkened veil to reveal more of My world to them. I trust them with My revelations and know that they will be used for My intended purpose.

Often My visionaries move others to pray for circumstances that are about to happen. Some tragedies are greatly lessened when prayer has been applied. Those who have been given this gift must pray that they use it rightly. They will receive confirmations through others as well as the Trinity. We, the Father, Son, and Holy Spirit, are one in thought. The Holy Spirit living within is your principal source of revelations.

Some visions will come but once. Others will occur over and over again. You are an ambassador to walk in the footsteps of Jesus. This position is one of high honor and esteem.

The people of the world will find your gift hard to believe but pay them no heed. You are in the world but not of the world.

Many of My righteous are working out their sanctification while on earth. Their wages for doing My work are high according to Heavenly standards but uncompensated according to earth's way of thinking.

Be of good courage, whatever your gifts. Use them for My honor and glory. Humbly embrace whatever cross comes your way.

Always be cheerful, to lift the spirits of others. This will do wonders for your own.

When I am generous to you, I expect you to be likewise to others. Pray for enlightenment as to the use of My gifts. Often I will speak through your Christian friends. You must seek confirmations from a number of sources for the evil one also puts ideas in people's heads.

Those who are given the gift of vision should praise and thank Me and more will be added. Along with the gift goes a great deal of responsibility. They should pray that they are ever in My will for its use.

There are times that I will let My faithful know that they are in My family by giving them glimpses of My face, but then it will be like looking through a glass darkly. Some will see a dove as a sign that I am with them. Others could see an angel's face or faces of people who need prayer.

Often I will put names in a person's mind and want prayers said for them. Some could be facing a dangerous situation brought about by Satan himself or his working demons.

There is real battle going on in the spiritual realm, so dress for it in the morning. Take up your shield (your salvation) and the sword of the Spirit (My word).

This is why it is so important to have a number of scriptures memorized. Repeating just the name of "Jesus" scatters the enemy.

If you have been blessed with visions, keep in prayer and you will receive more.

Often you can help others with My revelations through your visions. You can intercede in prayer for the souls of the faces or names I bring into your mind.

My faithful can do so much to further My Kingdom. You have been chosen by Me to accomplish My purpose. Be ready and willing to go forward in My name. I will supply the abilities.

When you see My white dove, you will know that I am with you and have another mission for you to accomplish. Keep on guard for all spiritual signs. I work in numerous ways through each individual. Meditate alone in prayer to know My will and be sure to test the spirits. The evil one will not answer the question, "Do you believe in the Son of God?" You may often hear, "I am the Alpha and the Omega, the beginning and the end." You are thus on safe ground.

There is so much for My children to learn. Be open to the Holy Spirit and do not quench His workings.

Time is of the essence in these last days. You have heard and observed the signs of the times. Thank Me for giving you spiritual eyes and ears.

You are walking in the light as I am in the light. Your counter-parts walk in darkness and cannot possibly understand your ways. Be not hurt but go boldly forward on your spiritual journey.

Learn all that you can of My ways to add a greater dimension to your ministry. Each one who has been given gifts has a ministry. These gifts are to be used for My purpose. You will be given insight of My will for you. Keep attuned by reading your Bible and listening for My still small voice. When you remain in My will you are not left unaided.

Be in constant control of your life and do not let the evil one take over. Do not pay attention to his negative words. He is a liar and deceiver. Fight back with My word. You will win as goodness over-comes evil.

My peace is with you when you learn how to fight your own battles. You can relax in My love knowing I am with you. Never will I leave or forsake you.

~~~

Tell others of My love. Some suffer greatly thinking that they can never be forgiven for what they have done. I am an ever forgiving, loving God. It only takes a contrite heart on the sinner's part. When people commit their life wholly to Me, they will experience the peace that only I can give. The world falls far short of this peace.

~~~

When you have been given one of My gifts, such as vision, keep in prayer and ask for more. I will not hold back My revelations through them. You will experience My spiritual world beyond your imagination. Greater faith will be added to what you have already acquired.

~~~

My grace will be sufficient for My faithful to carry on My work upon the earth. Your gifts are many and they are diversified. Use them for the good of mankind.

~~~

Your love for all should spur you on to new heights. One can reach new levels as one grows spiritually. Continue to advance along the road of life.

~~~

Praying for others will always bring back blessings to you. So there is no excuse for doing nothing.

~~~

If you keep your mind on things above, you will not wander far. The evil one will try all sorts of ways to distract you. Learn to recognize his distractions. Then cast him out in a stern way using My name. He will flee when he knows you mean and believe it.

~~~

When you receive a vision and do not understand it, come to Me in prayer and meditation for the meaning. Going to others for interpretation will often change the meaning and confuse you.

~~~

I often let My people see the white dove showing them that

the Holy Spirit is within them. This bolsters their beliefs tremendously.

Too many doubts that the evil one implants keep one from accomplishing one's real potential.

Talk to Me and let Me be your real friend. Friends tell one another all that happens. My ear does not get tired listening, and remember, I sleep not. I hear everything My loved ones say. This is a mystery to you but very natural to Me as I am of the supernatural world.

Pray that you may see My face and I, the Son of Man, will show My face to you. It will be like looking through a glass darkly, but you will know without a doubt that I hear you and answer your prayers.

Anyone who calls on Me will receive some kind of answer. I relate to My people in diverse ways. I can make your life interesting and meaningful.

Most people will not ask, for they have an unbelieving heart or they think that they are undeserving. Just let Me be the judge. I delight in pleasing My people who come to Me with a contrite heart. Those who believe will receive.

I am pouring out My power in these latter days to build up My church. Things you thought impossible are made possible through My power and grace. There is no excuse for lack of brain power. I supply all the needs when you work for Me. Your willingness brings about action on My part.

Showing your faith through good example is honored by Me. I will send people your way to be touched. My anointing will follow.

Everyone is concerned about the signs taking place in the world. It has all been predicted in My word. If you have a hard time understanding My word, pray to the Holy Spirit to enlighten your mind. He is always ready to distribute His gifts, one of which is understanding.

⸻

You can visualize with your spiritual mind many things that have taken place in My word. This is also a special gift that can be obtained with perseverance and prayer. The visionary realm can be opened up and used in many ways.

⸻

Your gifts must be shown to accomplish My purpose. Otherwise, you will lose them. Timidity will vanish when you speak boldly in My name.

⸻

I let My followers see slightly into the spiritual realm to let them know that I am with them. They are weak and need some proof. My apostle Thomas needed proof. To some, their faith is built up so strongly that they need no signs. Those who receive signs are no better in My sight than those who do not. So do not envy your neighbor.

⸻

I love all My children equally, but have the right to choose the amount of grace to be poured out upon them. If you are My child in the state of grace, sinless and having been forgiven for past sins, you have nothing to fear for you have been put under special protection.

⸻

Watch and pray at all times. You do not know the day or time of My return but I can say that we are drawing close to the end of the ages. Reading My word will give you many signs of the times. Prophecies are being fulfilled.

⸻

Ask for My anointing on everything that you do. Your work will not be in vain. I can turn hardships into blessings which will benefit you now and into eternity.

⸻

Do not give into moods that keep you down. The evil one is oppressing you. Ask for grace to rise above this state. He who asks will receive.

⸻

The unbelievers have a rough time. They do nothing about learning of Me and think that the Bible is nonsense. Pray for your friends and neighbors who are unbelievers. Witness to them and let your example show forth your light. You can win souls for Me with effort on your part.

If you have been given visions do not hesitate to tell them. They were given to you for a purpose. I will carry through your earnestness and open up ears to hear. Worry not what people think. If you are persecuted for My sake, rejoice. You are highly favored from above.

Our Lady of Light Publications

Our Lady of Light Publications is the communications voice of Our Lady of Light Foundation, a non-profit, tax exempt, religious association. The foundation is organized to financially assist Our Lady of Light Ministries and Our Lady of the Holy Spirit Center, a former seminary in Norwood, Ohio. Monies generated from the sale of publications flow through the foundation in its various support functions.

A great many people have contributed to the startup of Our Lady of Light Publications and are deserving of deepest thanks from those of us who such a short time ago were so new to publishing. This book is the third of an ongoing series covering topics we feel are rich and timely to Christian spirituality in today's world.

Publication activity is now ongoing, with several books in the works and scheduled for completion in the coming months. Larry Memering, publications editor, and Ken Hinchey, publications business director, have been in place for some time now. They continue their work in the organization's day-to-day publishing operations.

This book introduces the literary work of Miriam Grosjean to the OLLP audience. Miriam is a delightful person to know, conscientious in the handling of the words entrusted to her. We are confident that she and her messages will earn your enthusiastic endorsement.

Our Lady of Light Ministries encompasses a number of existing and planned spiritual activities. Most notable at this time are the support of the Marian movement within the priesthood, an area youth ministry, a speakers' bureau, a pilgrimage agenda and our outstanding Gospa Group. The latter is itself involved in such diverse activities as rosary and charismatic services, conferences, retreats, days of recollection, a youth prayer group and fund raising to refurbish Our Lady of the Holy Spirit Center.

Gerry Ross, President, Our Lady of Light Foundation

Other Publications Available From Our Lady of Light Publications

Personal Revelations of Our Lady of Light, edited by Gerald Ross. The original account of the appearance of Our Lady of Light at Cold Spring, Kentucky in 1992, the background and subsequent events. This book, in its fourth printing, contains beautiful messages from Our Lady and Our Lord.
128 pages.   Donation price $5.00

More Personal Revelations of Our Lady of Light, edited by Gerald Ross. Continuing the accounts of a Batavia, Ohio visionary, this book includes the ongoing messages from Our Lady of Light, as related in the first book, Personal Revelations of Our Lady of Light. Contains messages from Our Lady and Jesus to the visionary and other participants in the Marian activities at Our Lady of the Holy Spirit Center in Cincinnati, Ohio.
144 pages.   Donation price $5.00

Final Personal Revelations of Our Lady of Light, edited by Gerald Ross. This book describes experiences of the Batavia Visionary through December, 1993. Especially important are the visits of several priests to the Ohio field. The book presents certain rosary materials and priestly biographical information.
278 pages.   Donation price $7.00

Visitations, Volume 1, by Miriam Grosjean. Lessons in living, one for every day in the year, as dictated by Our Lord Himself. This bedside reader offers remarkable insights into what it means to grow in holiness.
128 pages   Donation Price $5.00

Insights and Counsels, Miriam Grosjean. Comments on the gifts and fruits of the Holy Spirit. 23 chapters, each developing the topic of one of the biblically sourced gifts or fruits. Words given to a well-known Dayton, Ohio locutionist. The book is popular for use at Life in the Spirit Seminars.
154 pages   Donation price $5.00

The above titles are available through religious bookstores or directly from the publisher:

Our Lady of Light Publications
P.O. Box 17541
Ft. Mitchell, KY 41017

OLLP is the publishing arm of Our Lady of Light Foundation, a non-profit association. Dedicated to fostering an increase in love of God in general and the causes of Mary, our mother, and Jesus, her Son, it supports its works entirely on donations such as those shown above. When ordering from the publisher, please add $1.50 for one book, total mailing cost not to exceed $10.00 per order in North America. Shipping charges outside North America are $5.00 U.S. for a single book; prevailing first class postage rates (unless specified otherwise), plus a nominal packing charge of $.25 per book, apply on larger quantities. Contact OLLP with any questions.